Iowa Northern Railway: History Through the Miles

Barton Jennings

Iowa Northern Railway: History Through the Miles
Copyright © 2024 by Barton Jennings

Publisher's Cataloging-in-Publication Data
Jennings, Barton

Iowa Northern Railway: History Through the Miles
264p.; 21cm.
ISBN: 979-8-9904307-0-9
Library of Congress Control Number: 2024937923

Front cover photo by Barton Jennings. IANR #461 at Shellsburg, Iowa.
Back cover photo by Sarah Jennings.
All interior photos by Barton Jennings unless otherwise noted.

Please send comments or corrections to sarah@techscribes.com

TechScribes, Inc.
PO Box 2199
Alma, AR 72921
www.techscribes.com

Printed in the United States of America

Map of Iowa Northern Railway Trackage

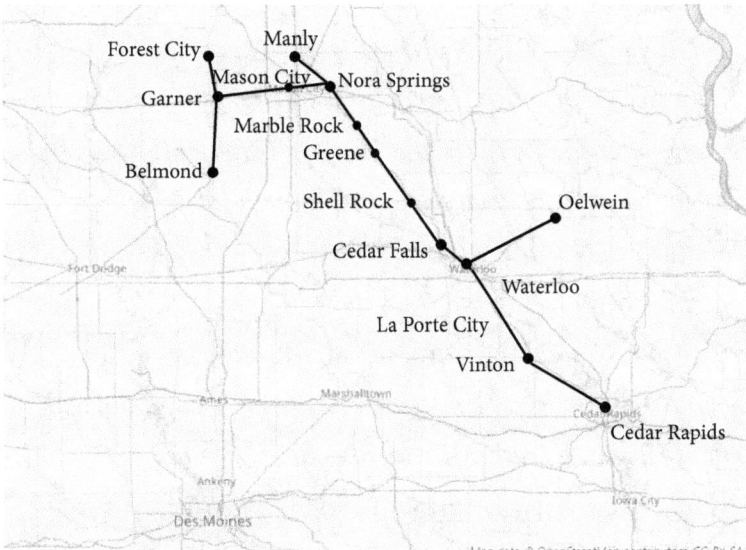

Map by Sarah Jennings. Based on 2024 100K Topo Map from the US Geological Survey.

Other books by Barton Jennings

<u>History Through the Miles</u>

Arkansas & Missouri Railroad: History Through the Miles

Alaska Railroad: History Through the Miles

Iowa Interstate Railroad: History Through the Miles

Everett Railroad: History Through the Miles

Tennessee Central Railway: History Through the Miles

Whitewater Valley Railroad: History Through the Miles

Oregon's Joseph Branch: History Through the Miles

Missouri & North Arkansas Railroad:
    History Through the Miles

Hennepin Canal Parkway: History Through the Miles

Idaho's Payette River Railroads: History Through the Miles

Delta Heritage Trail (Missouri Pacific's Wynne
    Subdivision): History Through the Miles

The Choctaw Route: History Through the Miles

The Railroads of U.S. Sugar: History Through the Miles

The Heavener Sub: History Through the Miles

The Little Rock: History Through the Miles

<u>Textbook</u>

*The Basics of Transportation: Policies, Practices and Pricing
– An Applied Perspective*

Contents

Creating an Iowa Northern Railway Route Guide

December 6, 2023 – CN today announced that it has signed and closed an agreement to acquire Iowa Northern Railway (IANR), which operates approximately 275 track miles in Iowa connecting to CN's U.S. rail network.

With this announcement, it became obvious that it was time to complete this route guide for a very successful railroad in Iowa. This book is designed to provide a guide to the route of the Iowa Northern Railway, once a mainline of the Chicago, Rock Island & Pacific. For several decades, the Iowa Northern Railway (IANR) has operated a limited number of excursion passenger trains over various parts of the railroad. This route description was first written in 2011-2012 for a series of passenger train charters, sponsored by different organizations, over various parts of the railroad. It has been updated since by several other visits to the company. Much of the information comes from internal railroad records, government and public records, railroad workers, and conversations with old and new friends. A number of these sources are listed in this book. In particular, the managers of Iowa Northern deserve a thanks for their help by reviewing and commenting on this book.

The railroad was mostly built by the Burlington, Cedar Rapids & Minnesota Railway Company, with the last few miles finished by the Burlington, Cedar Rapids & Northern Railway Company. It was part of the huge growth in railroad mileage across the Midwest during the late 1860s and 1870s. Its route was certainly described by the Burlington, Cedar Rapids & Minnesota Railway name. The Iowa Northern eventually operated the line that connected Cedar Rapids with Manly, just a few miles south of the Minnesota state line.

The tracks today look little like those built in the 1870s as the rail line has been improved numerous times over its more than 150 years. Hills have been cut down and bridges strengthened, stations and agents have been retired, and sidings have been removed and installed as needed. Even with these changes, much of the line's history can still be found along its route. There are several museums along the line, a number of stations and bridges, and lots of trains that can still be photographed.

There are a few reminders of the Rock Island Railroad along the Iowa Northern Railway. This Rock Island emblem can be found on the Vinton train depot, now used as the Vinton Depot Museum.

This work is based upon several earlier research projects on the railroad. This research has led to a collection of thousands of photographs and drawers full of railroad documents and company history. There is always the question about how much detail to provide in a book like this. While it cannot be the goal to include every detail about the line, there is an effort to explain the history of each community along the line, what shippers were located there, and what facilities the railroad had. Obviously, all of these changed over the more than one hundred years of the railroad's operating history, so the challenge is how much information to report. In writing this book, the author attempted to include information about the first few years of the railroad's existence, the improvements made by the Chicago, Rock Island & Pacific during the early 1900s, the peak of a community's activity, the railroad as it existed during the routine operations by the Rock Island, and what remained in 2023 as operated by the Iowa Northern Railway. Not everything is reported, but enough history is provided to give the reader an idea of what happened at each location.

The railroad historically used east-west as the line's description, although it actually operated southeast to northwest, and in many areas it curves greatly from these directions. This east-west direction was based upon train traffic to and from Chicago, the eastern end of the Chicago, Rock Island & Pacific.

Today, the Iowa Northern Railway uses south to north for the Cedar Rapids to Manly mainline. Therefore, this route description will be based upon the railroad's own terminology. A train heading from Cedar Rapids to Waterloo and on to Manly is heading north, so to the left is railroad-west, and to the right is railroad-east. Directions on other IANR lines are provided where needed. Note that every station and bridge location is also identified by a milepost location. Railroads identify locations along their routes by mileposts, much like highways do. For the Iowa Northern, most of the mileposts date back to the construction of the railroad, and their distance is from the former Rock Island station in Burlington, Iowa. The mileposts for each location are included in this guide. There are signs every mile along the railroad that identify this distance, so watch for them if you wish.

Additionally, the tracks were often described by their length in feet or car-lengths. These car-lengths varied over the years, but were generally around 45 feet per car. Therefore, a track listed as being 20 cars in length could hold about 900 feet of train. Many of the bridges have also been replaced or improved, so where timber trestles once stood, steel and concrete spans can now be found.

Another help in following the railroad and knowing what was at many of the locations are the many maps available on the internet. County road maps, topographic (topo) maps, and many other maps from the era can be found. Comparing these older maps with newer maps can often make finding the railroad easier. The U.S. Geological Survey has been very active making their Historical Topographic Map Collection available through TopoView. These maps are highly recommended and are far too numerous to reproduce in total in this book.

A final issue deals with all of the names that were used to represent parts of the railroad over its one-hundred-plus years. To simplify the issue, the term Chicago, Rock Island & Pacific or Rock Island will generally be used. Additionally, an ampersand (&) will be used in railroad company names to make them easier to identify. Especially with a company like the Burlington, Cedar Rapids & Minnesota Railway, mixing the railroad name and the cities that it served can get very confusing. Therefore, even if the firm did not use or always use an ampersand, one will be used in this book. Please forgive these simplifications.

Acknowledgments

The author has been fortunate enough to know some of the employees who worked for the railroad over the last several decades, and in a number of cases, ride across the railroad with them. Additionally, he has had the pleasure to get to know a number of the people who have researched the railroad. These all deserve a thanks for their help.

A number of documents were also used in writing this book. It is amazing what can be found on the internet these days. Copies of the *Official Guide*, the annual reports of various state railroad and corporation commissions, Interstate Commerce Commission reports, and other such documents were great resources. The Chicago, Rock Island & Pacific produced numerous documents that are still available. These include timetables, track charts, lists of stations, contracts, and even its own company magazine. Related sources such as the Goodspeed Publishing Company, Sanborn Insurance Maps, and others were a great aid. Newspapers also reported heavily on the construction and operations of the railroad. Finally, the author has a house with several rooms full of books, timetables and other documents about this and other railroads – important research items from a time long before today's internet.

It should be noted that this guide is not designed to be a complete history of the Iowa Northern Railway, but instead it provides a great deal of information for those who like to ask "where are we and what once happened here?" Because of this, the guide includes information about current as well as former station locations, historic towns, and major stream crossings along the line.

It is hoped that you enjoy your adventure with the Iowa Northern and that this book is of assistance in some ways – *Iowa Northern Railway: History Through the Miles*.

The Iowa Northern of 2023

The Iowa Northern Railway operates 167 miles in Iowa between Cedar Rapids, in eastern Iowa, and Manly in north central Iowa, and a total of 227 miles across Northeast Iowa. As stated by the *2017 Iowa State Rail Plan*, the "Iowa Northern Railway (IANR), based in Cedar Rapids and Manly, Iowa, is the state's largest Class III railroad and it operates a regional network consisting of approximately 167 miles of railroad it owns, leases, and operates under contract, all in Iowa." The 117 miles of track owned by the Iowa Northern represents 3.04% of the Iowa rail network.

The Iowa Northern Railway Company was formed in 1984 on a section of the old Chicago, Rock Island & Pacific Railroad Company. The railroad operates more than 160 miles of track that runs southeast to northwest from Cedar Rapids to Manly. The railroad also operates two branches reached via operating rights, a branch line from Waterloo east to Oelwein, and a branch line from Forest City south to Belmond, all within the state of Iowa.

The railroad connects with the Cedar Rapids & Iowa City Railway in Cedar Rapids; with the Canadian National Railway in Cedar Rapids and Waterloo; with the Canadian Pacific Railway in Nora Springs and Plymouth; and with the Union Pacific Railroad in Manly, Waterloo and Cedar Rapids. Until 2018, the railroad was headquartered in the old Paramount Theatre Building at 305 Second Street in Cedar Rapids. Iowa Northern also once had Customer Service and General Offices located in Greene and its Bryant Yard Shops located in Waterloo. In 2018, the company concentrated their offices in the Farmers State Bank building off West San Marnan Drive in Waterloo.

Iowa Northern Railway Founding

As stated, this railroad consists of track primarily once operated by the Chicago, Rock Island & Pacific Railroad. The Rock Island closed on March 31, 1980, leaving shippers along these lines without service. On August 7, 1981, service by several on-line shippers began between Cedar Rapids and Vinton and from Shell Rock to Nora Springs. The service opened the entire route in 1982, but the route was still owned by the estate of the bankrupt Chicago, Rock Island & Pacific Railroad.

A new company was created to own and operate the railroad, and in July 1984, the line from Cedar Rapids to Manly was sold to the newly created Iowa Northern Railway for $5.4 million. The Iowa Northern was originally owned by a group of on-line grain elevators, but was sold to Iron Road Railways (IRR) in 1994. Iron Road Railways owned several other railroads, including the Bangor & Aroostook Railroad, Canadian American Railroad, and the Windsor & Hantsport Railway. At the time, Daniel Sabin, a former employee of the Rock Island who had worked on this line, was an official with IRR.

Dan Sabin had a long history with the tracks and railroad that became the Iowa Northern Railway. First, his father, Art Sabin, worked for the Chicago, Rock Island & Pacific as an engineer from 1944 to 1976, many of those years out of Manly, Iowa. Dan's four older brothers also worked for the Rock Island in multiple positions, including as a clerk, signal maintainer, engineer and conductor. Dan Sabin started with the railroad as a student train order operator in August 1968 at the reported age of 15. He became a train dispatcher three years later, and then a night chief dispatcher a year later. After obtaining a college degree, he went to work for Canadian Pacific (CP), which explains the colors of the Iowa Northern locomotives. At CP, he worked as a trainmaster, assistant superintendent and director of service planning system before moving to the Chessie System in 1981, where he held several positions in operations. By 1987, Sabin had co-founded Transportation Operations Inc., a consulting services firm for small railroads, rail shippers, and state governments. In 1988, Transportation Operations began working with the Iowa Northern. Later, Sabin was involved with the creation of Iron Road Railways.

In 2002, IRR entered bankruptcy due to a great loss of business on its New England and Canadian operations, and the Iowa Northern was sold to former IRR director Daniel Sabin and a small group of investors. This allowed management to focus on the Iowa market and the shippers that had originally saved the railroad.

After the short line was established in 1984, the railroad handled 12,000 revenue cars and the average track speed was less than 10 mph. One of the important projects of the railroad has been to rebuild the track to allow the line to handle the tonnage required by most shippers. For years, the railroad plowed most of its profits back into the tracks and bridges. Some financing of track improvements has come from low-interest loans from the state of Iowa. The almost $6 million in loans were used to upgrade the track for higher speeds, and were repaid by selling the installed rails and then leasing them back from the Bank of Boston.

By 2006, traffic had surged to 40,000 revenue cars and the average track speed was 30 mph. However, after the 2008 floods, the railroad again had to rebuild much of the line and brought in The Andersons, Inc., in 2010 as a minority partner to raise additional cash. The Andersons operates grain elevators, ethanol plants, fertilizer facilities, and leases and repairs rail cars. This arrangement allowed The Andersons to obtain facilities on the railroad to manage and repair their railcar fleet, providing additional revenue to both parties.

Today, the traffic volumes have increased to more than 60,000 revenue cars a year. A major part of this traffic increase has been a change in the products that the railroad moves. In 2010, almost 75 percent of the railroad's revenue came from moving corn and soybeans. In 2016, these commodities only represent about 20 percent. Products such as ethanol, DDG (dry distillers grains), windmill components, farm equipment, fertilizers, and others have grown at a rapid pace and now make up a majority of the freight moved. Still, nearly 200 million bushels of grain, corn, and soybeans are cycled each year through the 17-county elevator system with a presence on the Iowa Northern. Most of the grain and corn traffic loaded along the IANR is destined for Cedar Rapids for processing into sweeteners, alcohol, and corn starch at plants operated by ADM and Cargill, or to the POET ethanol plants at Fairbank and Shell Rock.

The various ADM plants at Cedar Rapids are the destinations of many carloads of grain off of the Iowa Northern Railway.

Over the years, several agreements have expanded the reach of the Iowa Northern Railway. In 2003, the railroad obtained an agreement to operate the track owned by the D&W Railroad between Waterloo and Oelwein. The IANR acquired this line in 2020. It was solidified when the railroad also leased the Waterloo tracks of the Union Pacific Railroad Company in 2019.

In 2011, the Iowa Northern also expanded by getting approval to operate the Forest City Line, owned by North Central Iowa Rail Corridor. This line was a former Rock Island route between Belmond and Forest City, and it required trackage rights over today's Canadian Pacific to reach the isolated line.

Iowa Northern Railway Operations

According to the Iowa Northern Railway, 54% of the railroad's business is farm products, 23% is hazardous commodity, 8% is chemical and allied products, 7% is food and kindred products, 5% is machinery (except electrical), and 3% is all other commodities. To help grow a diversity in the products that the railroad hauls, it operates a series of transload terminals along the entire railroad. Some of these are at Waterloo, Bryant and Manly.

The Iowa Northern also benefits from a number of interchange locations with other railroads, providing connecting rail service across the country. This is especially important with the operations of container service to the west coast and to international customers. At the south end of the railroad at Cedar Rapids, the railroad interchanges with Union Pacific, Canadian National, the Cedar Rapids & Iowa City (CIC), and the Iowa Interstate via the CIC. At Waterloo, there is a direct interchange again with Canadian National. At Nora Springs, the Iowa Northern can interchange traffic with Canadian Pacific (now Canadian Pacific

Kansas City). Finally, at the north end of the railroad, Manly is an important interchange point with Union Pacific.

Iowa Northern trains, crews and locomotives can be found just about anywhere at any time along the railroad. However, IANR crews are primarily based out of Bryant and Waterloo. Crews out of Bryant handle the Waterloo–Manly segment using one or more sets of locomotives, normally two to three units each. Generally, there are three crews working three shifts daily (7am, 3pm, and 11pm), taking a company vehicle out to the train wherever it happens to be when their tour of duty begins. There is also generally a crew at Manly and/or Bryant to handle local customers and switching.

For service south of Waterloo, a crew is called most evenings at Bryant Yard to make a run to Cedar Rapids, arriving there sometime between midnight and 2am. This crew often gets relieved at Cedar Rapids between 3am and 5am and comes back north to Bryant Yard. If time permits, they also operate a transfer to the UP Linden Yard at Waterloo prior to a late-morning tie up. Four to five locomotives are used on this normally long and heavy tonnage train. When the Fairbank ethanol plant was opened, train service to Oelwein was expanded from a once-per-week routine to every day. A crew is called to work late mornings at Bryant Yard for the run to Fairbank, and operates to Oelwein as needed, usually on Tuesday and Thursday, although Saturday service has been known to happen. Several yard crews are also assigned to the yard and transload complex at Manly. The crew normally operates during daylight hours Monday through Saturday.

IANR Passenger Trains

Besides the freight trains, the Iowa Northern also operated passenger trains. In 2006, the Iowa Northern purchased six former C&NW/Metra Chicago bi-level commuter cars and a former Amtrak F40PHR locomotive for their *Hawkeye Express* train, which actually started operations in 2004. The *Hawkeye Express* was a train designed to haul people to University of Iowa football games in Iowa City from satellite parking areas to the west of town. The *Hawkeye Express* operated multiple trips before and after the game, generally starting three to four hours before the game, and then for about 90 minutes after the game. The train could hold around 1300 people. Over the years, the train handled an average of 5000 passengers to the game. The train operated on the Iowa Interstate, but some special trips are made on the Iowa Northern. The last *Hawkeye Express* trips were made during the 2019 football season.

The cars used by the *Hawkeye Express* are former Metra cars from Chicago commuter service. There were all built as bilevel cars for the Chicago & North Western commuter service on the west and north sides of Chicago. The cars include five coaches built 1960-61 by Pullman, and one coach/cab car built by Pullman in 1960. The coach/cab car can be used to lead the train with locomotives pushing from the other end.

IANR 7704	ex-Metra 7704	ex-CNW 53	coach
IANR 7723	ex-Metra 7723	ex-CNW 72	coach
IANR 7735	ex-Metra 7735	ex-CNW 84	coach
IANR 7743	ex-Metra 7743	ex-CNW 92	coach
IANR 7750	ex-Metra 7750	ex-CNW 99	coach
IANR 8704	ex-Metra 8704	ex-CNW 155	coach/cab

Passenger cars like this one were used through the 2019 football season on the *Hawkeye Express* trains that served the University of Iowa.

Iowa Northern Locomotives

For a relatively small railroad, the Iowa Northern has had a wide variety of locomotives, from traditional freight engines to former passenger engines to specialized slug units. Additionally, the railroad has several historic passenger locomotives used for special events. Most were built by EMD, the Electro-Motive Division of General Motors, now Electro-Motive Diesel which is a part of Progress Rail Services, owned by Caterpillar. The three former Canadian National locomotives were built by General Motors Diesel (GMD), the Canadian division of EMD.

The only locomotives not built by EMD are the various slugs and MP Genset units. The slugs are units which do not have a diesel engine. Instead, they use electricity produced by another locomotive, an especially effective practice at lower speeds. These slugs were built by the Atchison, Topeka & Santa Fe (ATSF). The MP1500D and MP2000D Genset units were built by Motive Power Industries. They have low horsepower engines and can obtain peak power from a series of batteries. Both the slugs and the MP loco-motives were built using the frames of older EMD locomotives.

Putting together a locomotive roster for the Iowa Northern can be a tricky subject as a number of locomotives have come and gone. An example is this 2014 photo of CIT #3800 and IANR #3811, posed side-by-side in Bryant Yard in Waterloo, Iowa.

The heart of the Iowa Northern's locomotive fleet are 12 rebuilt GP38-2s, #3800-3811, all of which wear the road's attractive paint scheme, patterned after Canadian Pacific's classic Tuscan red and gray livery. These engines were originally leased from Locomotive Leasing Partners (LLPX), but IANR has been working toward purchasing all 12. All were originally constructed for the Louisville & Nashville in 1971, except for the #3800, which began its career in 1970 as Baltimore & Ohio #4812 and the #3801, which came to life as Penn Central #7935.

To help out with increased business, three reconditioned GP40-2Ws were received in spring 2007 from dealer Progress Rail Services. They were built in 1974 for CN and carry the wide-nose Canadian Safety Cab. Their new numbers are #4001 (CN 9425), #4002 (CN 9445), and #4003 (CN 9508). The railroad also has several slugs, introduced in July 2010.

The Iowa Northern has also received several former Amtrak locomotives. To make them more suitable for freight service, these former passenger units were previously modified by the addition of a front "porch" that makes it easier for crews riding the units during switching movements. In addition, the HEP (head end power) alternator has been removed. Dubbed F40M-2F, they were obtained from the Canadian American Railroad (CDAC), which bought them from Amtrak. They retain their CDAC numbers and continue to wear the old Canadian Pacific inspired livery that IANR adopted from the old Iron Road operations. F40PHR #678 has historically been used on the *Hawkeye Express* passenger trains. Recently, #461 was rebuilt by MidAmerica in Kansas City and had a new HEP system installed to also handle passenger trains on the railroad.

In addition to the locomotives used for freight service, there are two historic locomotives that once operated for the Chicago, Rock Island & Pacific. Both are former passenger locomotives, designated as E-series locomotives by EMD. These two locomotives are assigned to the Manly Junction Railroad Museum, but are often displayed at special events across the railroad. Information about these two locomotives, #630 and #652, are included here.

Number	Serial Model	Build Number	Date	Notes
451	F40PHR	777107-11	7/1979	

Built as Amtrak #314, to Canadian American #451, to Montreal, Maine & Atlantic #451, to Iowa Northern #451

Number	Serial Model	Build Number	Date	Notes
454	F40PHR	807050-24	7/1981	

Built as Amtrak #384, to Canadian American #454, to Iowa Northern #454

458　　　F40PHR　　807038-1　　12/1980
Built as Amtrak #360, to Canadian American #458, to Iowa Northern #458

461　　　F40PHR　　777018-12　　12/1977
Built as Amtrak #266, to Canadian American #461, to Iowa Northern #461

630　　　E6A　　　1424　　　10/1941
Built as Chicago, Rock Island & Pacific #630, to private owner and stored at Midland Railway in Kansas, to Dan Sabin as CRIP #630

652　　　E8A　　　15199　　　3/1952
Built as Chicago, Rock Island & Pacific #652, served as CRIP Bicentennial unit, to private owner and stored at Midland Railway in Kansas, to Dan Sabin as CRIP #652

678　　　F40PH　　777001-12　　9/1977
Built as Amtrak #241, to Ferromex #241, to Iowa Northern #678, scrapped late 2023

1501　　MP1500D
Built as Denver & Rio Grande Western #5932 (GP9, sn 22069, 7/1956), to Austin & Northwestern #55, rebuilt by MPI to MP1500D demonstrator MPEX #1501, to New Orleans Public Belt #1501, to New Orleans Public Belt #2008, to Iowa Northern #1501

1502　　MP1500D
Built as Southern Pacific #5669 (GP9, sn 21362, 4/1956), to Southern Pacific #3502, to Southern Pacific 3434 (2nd), to Louisiana & Delta #3434, to Louisiana & Delta #1751, rebuilt by MPI to MP1500D demonstrator MPEX #1502, to Iowa Northern #1502

2000　　GP20　　27354　　　4/1962
Built as Southern Pacific #7233, rebuilt to Southern Pacific #4101, to Iowa Northern #2000, retired, placed on display at Manly, Iowa

2001   GP20   27108   3/1962
Built as Southern Pacific #7221, rebuilt to Southern Pacific
#4150, to Iowa Northern #2001, retired
2002   GP20   26305   12/1960
Built as St. Louis Southwestern #801, rebuilt to Southern
Pacific #4140, to Iowa Northern #2002, retired
2003   GP20   26304   12/1960
Built as St. Louis Southwestern #800, rebuilt to Southern
Pacific #4144, to Iowa Northern #2003, retired

On January 5, 1997, Iowa Northern #2003 was teamed with Chicago
& North Western #4201 while working North Yard at Cedar Rapids.

2004   MP2000D
Built by MPI to MP2000D demonstrator MPEX #2004, to
Iowa Northern #2004
2005   MP2000D
Built by MPI to MP2000D demonstrator MPEX #2005, to
Iowa Northern #2005
2492   GP7   A167   ?/1951
Built as Chesapeake & Ohio #5733, to Iowa Northern
#2492, retired

2493   CF7   8712   10/1949
Built as ATSF #300L (F7A), renumbered #300, rebuilt to ATSF #2493 (CF7), to Arkansas Midland #493, to Iowa Northern #2493, to Florida Central #48

3607   GP38   35427   10/1969
Built as Penn Central #7798, to Conrail #7798, to Chicago, Missouri & Western #7798, renumber #2038, to Helm Leasing HLCX #3607, leased to Iowa Northern #3607, lease ended in 2007

3609   GP38   35439   10/1969
Built as Penn Central #7810, to Conrail #7810, to Chicago, Missouri & Western #7810, renumber #2045, to Helm Leasing HLCX #3609, leased to Iowa Northern #3609, lease ended in 2007

3800   GP38-2   36688   9/1970
Built as Baltimore & Ohio #4812, to CSX #2112, to LLPX #2026, to Iowa Northern #3800

3801   GP38-2   36990   3/1971
Built as Penn Central #7935, to Conrail #7935, to CSX #1996, to LLPX #2022, to Iowa Northern #3801

3802   GP38-2   37275   5/1971
Built as Louisville & Nashville #4037, to Seaboard System #6258, to CSX #2167, to LLPX #2157, to Iowa Northern #3802

3803   GP38-2   37633   6/1971
Built as Louisville & Nashville #4044, to Seaboard System #6265, to CSX #2174, to LLPX #2152, to Iowa Northern #3803

3804   GP38-2   37632   6/1971
Built as Louisville & Nashville #4043, to Seaboard System #6264, to CSX #2173, to LLPX #2160, to Iowa Northern #3804

3805   GP38-2   37268   5/1971
Built as Louisville & Nashville #4030, to Seaboard System #6251, to CSX #2160, to LLPX #2155, to Iowa Northern #3805

3806   GP38-2   37277   5/1971
Built as Louisville & Nashville #4039, to Seaboard System #6260, to CSX #2169, to LLPX #2158, to Iowa Northern #3806

3807   GP38-2   35977   5/1971
Built as Louisville & Nashville #4023, to Seaboard System #6244, to CSX #2153, to LLPX #2159, to Central Oregon & Pacific #5153, to Indiana & Ohio #5153, to Iowa Northern #3807

3808   GP38-2   35975   5/1971
Built as Louisville & Nashville #4021, to Seaboard System #6242, to CSX #2151, to LLPX #2151, to Iowa Northern #3808

3809   GP38-2   35978   5/1971
Built as Louisville & Nashville #4024, to Seaboard System #6245, to CSX #2154, to LLPX #2153, to Iowa Northern #3809

3810   GP38-2   35974   5/1971
Built as Louisville & Nashville #4020, to Seaboard System #6241, to CSX #2150, to LLPX #2150, to Iowa Northern #3810

3811   GP38-2   35983   5/1971
Built as Louisville & Nashville #4029, to Seaboard System #6250, to CSX #2159, to CSX #9653, to LLPX #2160, to Iowa Northern #3811

Iowa Northern #3811 was working Bryant Yard in 2014 preparing for the run to Cedar Rapids that night.

3951   slug
Built as Union Pacific #345 (GP9, sn 23701, 9/1957), rebuilt to ATSF #105 (4th), to ATSF #1105 (2nd), to BNSF #3954, to Iowa Northern #3951

3952   slug
Built as ATSF #1111 (GP20, sn 25584, 10/1960), rebuilt to ATSF #109 (3rd), to ATSF #1109 (2nd), to BNSF #3958, to Iowa Northern #3952

3953   slug
Built as Union Pacific #143B (GP9B, sn 19219, 2/1954), rebuilt to ATSF #117 (2nd), to ATSF #1117 (2nd), to BNSF #3961, to Iowa Northern #3953

3954   slug
Built as Union Pacific #116 (GP7, sn 18575, 8/1953), rebuilt to ATSF #118 (2nd), to ATSF #1118 (2nd), to BNSF #3962, to Iowa Northern #3954

3955   slug

Built as New York Central #5653 (GP7, sn 14215, 9/1951), to Penn Central #5653, to Conrail #5653, rebuilt to ATSF #106 (4th), to ATSF #1106 (2nd), to BNSF #3955, to Iowa Northern #3955

Iowa Northern #3955 was one of several slugs (unpowered locomotives) that were acquired by the railroad to help move heavy trains at slower speeds across the property.

3956   slug

Built as Pennsylvania #8550 (GP7, sn 18665, 9/1953), to Pennsylvania #5850, Penn Central #5850, to Penn Central #5884, to Conrail #5884, rebuilt to ATSF #107 (4th), to ATSF #1107 (2nd), to BNSF #3956, to Iowa Northern #3956

4001   GP40-2LW   A3003   5/1974
Built as Canadian National #9425, to Iowa Northern #4001
4002   GP40-2LW   A3023   6/1974
Built as Canadian National #9445, to Iowa Northern #4002

IANR #4002 is parked in front of the Bryant Yard shops at Waterloo with two recently acquired slugs.

4003   GP40-2LW   A3086   9/1974
Built as Canadian National #9508, to Iowa Northern #4003
4100   GP40-3   ?   ?
New to roster during 8/2023; wears IANR Red, Gray & Gold
9016   GP10   18813   5/1954
Built as Illinois Central #9016 (GP9), to Illinois Central Gulf #9016, to Cedar Valley Railroad #9016, to Iowa Northern #9016, retired

Besides locomotives, the Iowa Northern also rostered a few cabooses like #11, shown at Waterloo in 2010.

Cedar Rapids to Manly Junction

Logo of the Iowa Route of the Burlington, Cedar Rapids & Northern Railway, from *Travelers' Official Guide of the Railway and Steam Navigation Lines in the United States and Canada*, June 1893, page 541.

MAIN LINE.

3	5	1	61	Mls.	May 14, 1893.	Mls.	2	6	4	18
*8 45	*1230	*8 45			lve.... St. Louis ..arr.	464.0		*3 00	*6 30	
P.M.	NO'N	P.M.			(St.L.K.& Nor.W.Ry.)			P.M.	A.M.	
	*1245				lve....Chicago...arr.	460.0	8 20			
	NO'N				(Chic. Burl.& Q. R.R.)		A.M.			
	*3 50	*1030	1030		lve....Chicago....arr.	412.0	*7 15	*11 15		*715
	P.M.	P.M.	P.M		(Chic. R. I. & Pac. Ry.)		A.M.	A.M		A.M.
A.M.	P.M.	A.M.			LEAVE] [ARRIVE		N'HT	A.M.	P.M.	
	*8 15			.c	+....Burlington 1 ..ठ	252.7		7 15		
+8 40	8 25	+5 20		...	..Jefferson St. Depot ठ	....	12 35	7 05	7 00	
8 56				8.7	.........Latty........	244.0	12 16	6 45	6 44	
9 03		5 41		11.6	.........Sperry....ठ	241.1	12 09	6 36	6 38	
9 10	8 55	5 50		15.3	......Mediapolis.....ठ	237.4	12 00	6 29	6 30	
9 20				19.9	.........Linton.....ठ	232.8	11 49	6 17	6 21	
9 26	9 08	6 10		22.7	+...Morning Sun 2.ठ	230.0	11 42	6 10	6 15	
9 40	9 20	6 22		29.3	.....Wapello ....ठ	223.4	11 27	5 56	6 02	
9 54				35.2	.......Bard ......ठ	217.5	11 13	5 45	5 50	
10 05	9 45	6 45		40.6	+..Columbus Junc.3.ठ	212.1	11 02	5 35	5 40	
10 15				44.6	......Port Allen......ठ	208.1			5 27	
10 20		6 56		47.6	.......Cone.......ठ	206.1	10 48	5 20	5 20	
10 40	10 10	7 12	A.M	55.0	......Nichols 4......ठ	197.7	10 38	5 04	5 05	P.M
...	10 30	7 25	*645	51.5	+...West Liberty 5.ठ	191.2	10 25	4 45	...	7 40
...			6 57	67.1	....Center Dale....ठ	185.6				7 27
...	10 45	7 42	7 05	69.8	...West Branch ...ठ	182.9	10 00	4 29	...	7 21
...			7 12	73.3	.......Oasis.....ठ	179.4				7 14
12 01	10 53	7 52	7 16	74.8	.......Elmira 6.....ठ	178.8	9 50		3 40	7 10
12 06			7 23	77.5	......Morse .....ठ	175.2	9 44		3 35	7 00
12 16			7 32	82.3	......Solon.....ठ	170.4	9 33		3 25	6 50
12 29			7 50	89.4	........Ely .....ठ	163.3	9 18		3 10	6 35
+1250	11 40	+8 40	8 10	98.1	arr..Cedar Rapids 7 ठ lve.	154.6	9 00	3 35	+2 50	*615
1 35	11 59	9 00	A.M.	98.1	lve.+.Cedar Rapids..arr.	154.6	+8 40	3 20	10 10	P.M.
1 45		9 10		102.3	........Linn .....ठ	150.4			10 00	
1 55		9 20		108.0	.........Palo .....ठ	144.7	8 18		9 50	
2 05		9 30		112.0	....Shellsburg.....ठ	140.7	8 10		9 40	
2 30	12 45	9 50		121.0	......Vinton 8.....ठ	131.7	7 50	2 39	9 10	
2 43		10 05		128.9	...Mount Auburn...ठ	123.8	7 35		8 52	
3 02	1 12	10 16		135.1	+......La Porte...ठ	117.6	7 20	2 13	8 40	
3 21		10 32		143.3	......Washburn.....ठ	111.1	7 05		8 25	
3 40	1 45	10 50		150.6	+....Waterloo 9.....ठ	102.1	6 50	1 45	8 08	
3 55	1 55	11 00		156.4	+..Cedar Falls 10.ठ	96.3	6 33	1 30	7 56	
4 11		11 15		164.7	....Winslow......ठ	88.0	6 15		7 40	
4 20	2 20	11 20		167.7	..Waverly Junction..	84.7	6 08	1 06	+7 35	
P.M.	2 30	11 30		172.0	+....Shell Rock.....ठ	80.7	6 00	1 00	A.M.	
	2 44	11 42		179.0	+...Clarksville 11..ठ	73.7	5 44	12 48		
	...	11 50		184.4	........Roots. ....ठ	68.3	5 30			
	3 05	12 02		190.0	+........Greene.......ठ	62.7	5 20	12 32		
	3 17	12 14		195.7	.....Marble Rock ...ठ	57.0	5 07	12 21		
	3 35	12 30		203.7	+.......Rockford.....ठ	49.0	4 59	12 07		
	3 50	12 45		210.9	+...Nora Junc. 12 .ठ	41.8	4 30	11 47		
	...	12 57		216.6	.......Rock Falls ....ठ	36.1	4 15			
		1 05		219.7	...Plymouth Junc.13..ठ	33.0	4 10			
		1 15		225.0	...Manly Junc.14..ठ	27.7	3 53			
		1 26		229.6	....Kensett.......ठ	23.1	3 48			
	4 41	1 40		236.0	...Northwood....ठ	16.7	3 35	11 02		
	...	1 52		241.1	......Gordonsville....ठ	11.6	3 23			
	...	2 02		245.7	......Glenville..ठ	7.0	3 14			
	5 13	2 20		252.7	+...Albert Lea 15..ठ	.0	+3 00	*1035		
	A.M.	P.M.			ARRIVE] [LEAVE		P.M.	P.M.		
	8 40	6 40		360.0	arr..Minneapolis.lve.		+10 25	*7 00		
	9 15	7 20		372.0	.......St. Paul....		+9 50	*6 25		
	A.M.	P.M.			ARRIVE] [LEAVE		A.M.	P.M.		

Schedule for the Burlington, Cedar Rapids & Northern Railway, from *Travelers' Official Guide of the Railway and Steam Navigation Lines in the United States and Canada*, June 1893, page 541.

MAIN LINE

Footage Capacity of		Station Numbers	SUBDIVISION 10 STATIONS TIME TABLE NO. 9 AUG. 21, 1977	Miles from Burlington	Signs
Sidings	Other Tracks				
......	Yard	52097	CEDAR RAPIDS YARD *TO(N)	98.1	RFWT BCYd
			— 3.6 —		
......	......	53102	LINN JCT......................P	101.7	Yd
			— 5.6 —		
3615	763	53108	PALO............................P	107.3	....
			— 4.1 —		
......	W1100	53112	SHELLSBURG.............. P	111.4	....
			— 9.6 —		
3130	4922	53121	VINTON......................TO	121.0	R
			— 0.2 —		
......	......	....	VINTON JCT..................P	121.2	Yd
			— 7.7 —		
......	800	53129	MOUNT AUBURN .... P	128.9	....
			— 6.4 —		
3095	3165	53135	LA PORTE CITY.......... P	135.3	....
			— 8.0 —		
	1600	53143	WASHBURN .... P	143.3	....
			— 4.9 —		
4634	Yard	53149	BRYANT........................P	148.2	Yd
			— 2.0 —		
......	......	....	CNW Crossing................A	150.2	....
			— 0.2 —		
......	Yard	53151	WATERLOO ....TO	150.4	CBYd
			0.6		
......	......	....	ICG Crossing A	151.0	....
			4.1		
......	......	....	CNW Crossing ....UX	156.2	....
			0.3		
1272	1233	53156	CEDAR FALLS.............. P	156.5	W
			1.0		
......	......	....	ICG Crossing .... AP	157.5	....
			— 14.6 —		
3411	2583	53172	SHELL ROCK .... P	172.1	....
			— 6.8 —		
......	......	....	CNW Crossing..................A	178.9	....
			— 0.1 —		
5279	1621	53179	CLARKSVILLE......... P	179.0	....
			— 6.1 —		
......	W1300	53186	PACKARD......................P	185.1	....
			— 4.9 —		
......	2500	53190	GREENE.......................TO	190.0	
			— 5.7 —		
3965	1695	53196	MARBLE ROCK .... P	195.7	....
			— 8.0 —		
......	3250	53204	ROCKFORD ....TO	203.7	
			— 7.2 —		
......	......	....	CMStP&P Crossing ....A	210.7	....
			— 0.2 —		
3204	237	53211	NORA SPRINGS...............P	211.0	....
			— 5.4 —		
......	W500	53217	ROCK FALLS.................P	216.4	....
			— 3.1 —		
......	......	....	CMStP&P Crossing ....UX	219.5	....
			— 0.0 —		
......	E250	53220	PLYMOUTH....................P	219.5	....
			— 5.3 —		
......	......	....	CNW Crossing................M	224.8	....
			— 0.3 —		
......	Yard	57225	MANLY ....*TO(N)	225.1	RFWT BC Yd
			127.2		

Automatic Block System - MP 98.1 to 225.1

Schedule for Subdivision 10, from the Rock Island's *Illinois Division Timetable No. 9,* August 21, 1977, page 24.

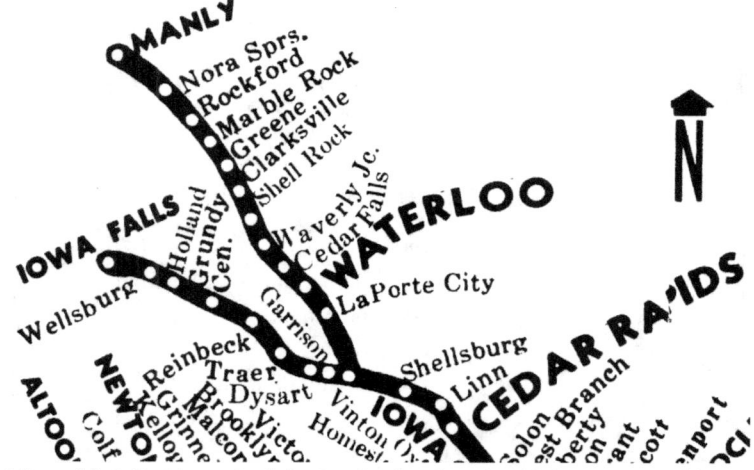

Map of Subdivision 10 of the Rock Island Railroad from *Timetable No. 1,* March 18, 1979, page 2.

The Iowa Northern Railway route from Cedar Rapids to Manly Junction includes two subdivisions, the **Cedar Rapids Subdivision** and the **Manly Subdivision.** These subdivisions include almost 120 miles of former Chicago, Rock Island & Pacific Railway, plus several miles of Union Pacific tracks in Cedar Rapids, and Canadian National tracks in the Waterloo-Cedar Falls area to connect the two subdivisions together.

The Iowa Northern Railway route between Cedar Rapids and Manly has an interesting history, with elements common to many other granger railroads. The oldest part of the line was built in the late 1860s by the Cedar Rapids & Saint Paul Railway Company, incorporated on October 2, 1865. It was incorporated "for the purpose of constructing, owning and operating a railroad and branches extending northwesterly from Cedar Rapids in the County of Linn in the State of Iowa, up the Cedar Valley in said State." The purpose of the line was to connect the farms and communities along the Cedar River to the Chicago, Iowa & Nebraska Railroad, which connected Chicago to the new

Union Pacific at Council Bluffs. However, the line was only built from Cedar Rapids to Vinton, Iowa, (24 miles) via Linn Junction, Palo, Shellsburg, and Greasers.

A second railroad was chartered on October 7, 1867, "to construct and operate a railroad extending from Cedar Rapids to Burlington, via Iowa City, via Wapello, to connect with a road from Burlington via Keokuk and St. Louis." This railroad, the Cedar Rapids & Burlington Railroad Company, never built any track. However, its charter was consolidated with the Cedar Rapids & Saint Paul Railway, creating the Burlington, Cedar Rapids & Minnesota Railway Company on June 30, 1868.

The Burlington, Cedar Rapids & Minnesota Railway Company (BCR&M) was created to "consolidate the Cedar Rapids and Burlington Railroad Company and the Cedar Rapids and St. Paul Railway into one organization; to acquire all the franchises, property and rights of both of said Companies; to locate, construct, maintain and operate a railway with double and single track and with all necessary branches, fences, bridges, warehouses, elevators, steamboats, lands and such other appendages as may be deemed necessary for the convenient use and profitable management of the same, from the City of Burlington, via Wapello, West Branch, Cedar Rapids, Vinton and Waterloo, to and into the State of Minnesota." This new railroad looked to connect business from along the Cedar River to multiple railroads to Chicago, as well as Mississippi River steamboat service at Burlington, Iowa.

Construction started from Burlington, Iowa, in early 1869, and the line reached Columbus Junction (41 miles of track) by the end of 1870, and Cedar Rapids (98 miles) in late 1871. Additionally, the railroad extended the line from Vinton to Waterloo by Christmas of the same year. In 1872, the line was further extended to Plymouth Junction. However, all construction stopped by September 1873 due to a financial panic, and the company defaulted on its bonds during November 1873. The Financial Panic of 1873 was triggered by a number of factors, including speculation in the railroad industry and the Coinage Act of 1873, which changed the national silver policy. The economic depression in the United States lasted until 1877.

By this time, the BCR&M was an important railroad, serving many Iowa shippers who would otherwise be captive to only one railroad, or have no rail service at all. However, the railroad was still too small with too few outside connections for the BCR&M to attract overhead traffic. The railroad had to be completed to survive. On May 19, 1875, the railroad fell into receivership, and during June 1876, was sold to the Burlington, Cedar Rapids & Northern Railway Company (BCR&N). The Burlington, Cedar Rapids & Northern Railway Company of Iowa was incorporated in June 1868 "to carry into effect a plan heretofore adopted for the reorganization of the Burlington, Cedar Rapids and Minnesota Railway Company." The railroad finished the line from Plymouth Junction to Manly, Iowa, (5 miles) by July 5, 1877. This allowed overhead traffic to flow out of Minnesota. With several connections to Chicago, the BCR&N was able to negotiate favorable rate divisions for this traffic, making the railroad very profitable.

This profit made the BCR&N the target of several purchase plans. On July 15, 1885, the railroad became controlled by the Chicago, Rock Island & Pacific Railway Company through majority stock purchase. This allowed the company to direct most of the Minnesota and northern Iowa traffic to its mainline at West Liberty, and then over the CRIP mainline to Chicago. This volume of traffic was so great that the CRIP was forced to make their mainline between Chicago and West Liberty double track and signaled.

Since the BCR&N wasn't totally owned by the CRIP, there was still the issue of complete control of this business. On June 1, 1902, the railroad was leased to the Chicago, Rock Island & Pacific Railway Company for 999 years. Finally, on June 15, 1903, the BCR&N was sold to the Chicago, Rock Island & Pacific Railway Company. As the Rock Island system matured, this route became a key component of the system, hosting numerous freights, especially during the harvest season.

This Rock Island emblem can be found on the D. C. Taylor Company office building at the south end of North Yard at Cedar Rapids, Iowa. The building was never owned by the Rock Island, but its builder wanted to note the railroad's presence.

The route may be most famous for being part of the route of the *Zephyr Rocket*, a passenger train jointly operated by the Chicago, Burlington & Quincy and the Rock Island between St. Louis and Minneapolis/St. Paul, Minnesota. Because of this, much of the line was double tracked and signalized. Although the last *Zephyr Rocket* operated on April 8, 1967, the line remained under ABS (Automatic

Block Signaling) control until the end of the Rock Island in 1980. For example, the CRIP *Illinois Division Employee Timetable #9* (August 21, 1977) indicated that ABS signals were in effect from Milepost 97.6 at Cedar Rapids, to Milepost 225.1 at Manly.

CRIP's *Central Division Employee Time Table No. 2*, dated October 30, 1966, showed the Cedar Rapids to Manly route as being very busy. Labeled as Subdivision 16, the route featured the daily #190 (eastbound) and #201 westbound passenger trains. #201 was scheduled to depart Cedar Rapids at 1:52am and arrive at Manly at 5:30am, stopping at almost all stations along the route. #190 operated in the reverse direction, leaving Manly at 7:10pm and arriving at Cedar Rapids at 10:05pm for a twenty-minute stop. The timetable also showed a number of second-class freight trains operating over part or all of the line. In 1973, the CRIP route from Cedar Rapids to Manly was shown as Subdivision 10, a mainline of the Northern Division. By 1979, the route was designated a branchline, Subdivision 10 of the Illinois Division.

In 1965, the Chicago, Rock Island & Pacific earned its final profit and the company survived off of previous profits, borrowed money, and sold assets. The railroad abandoned a number of branch lines, but the slow process of the Interstate Commerce Commission meant it could take years for actions to be taken. The result was that the Rock Island Railroad entered bankruptcy in 1975.

Attempted savings led to salaries and working conditions being lower than many of the more prosperous railroads, and in August 1979, the Rock Island clerks went on strike. With no one to do the paperwork, and the operating unions refusing to cross the picket lines, the railroad was basically shut down. Despite President Carter's order to return to work, strikers remained on the picket lines. Management soon was operating trains, serving as much as half of the previous volumes and actually turning a profit. However, with a concern about the cash available and the long-term future of the property, Bankruptcy Judge Frank J. McGarr ordered the railroad liquidated in January 1980, the largest liquidation of any American company to that point. Trains stopped running in early 1980, except for a few runs to move equipment to sale or scrapping locations. Soon, the Interstate Commerce Commission (ICC) had the Kansas City Terminal and its numerous owners operate the core of the railroad, a plan that lasted until March 23, 1980. After that, railroads began to lease or buy sections of track for operations from the Rock Island estate. Additionally, a few railroads were issued service orders by the ICC. However, the Rock Island Railroad of old was gone.

Train service on the Cedar Rapids-Manly line ended almost immediately, but on August 7, 1981, service by several on-line shippers began between Cedar Rapids and Vinton and from Shell Rock to Nora Springs. The service opened the entire route in 1982, but the route was still owned by the estate of the bankrupt Chicago, Rock Island & Pacific Railroad. The line was sold in July 1984 to the Iowa Northern Railway for $5.4 million. The Iowa Northern was originally owned by a group of on-line grain elevators, but was sold to Iron Road Railways (IRR) in 1994. This firm entered bankruptcy in 2002 and the Iowa Northern was sold to former IRR director Daniel Sabin. The *2017 Iowa State Rail Plan* states that the Iowa Northern includes the "principal route of the former CRI&P from Manly, Iowa, to Waterloo and Cedar Rapids, Iowa," and this former Rock Island mainline is still an important core of Iowa's largest Class III railroad.

Along this route, the railroad was built and then upgraded over the years with three main types of bridges, consisting of through plate girder (TPG), deck plate girder (DPG), and through truss spans. A TPG span consists of two vertical plates consisting of I-beams and steel plates to create a structural "wall." These plates support the bridge deck, and the tracks pass between the plates. A common name for the design is a pony girder since the tops of the plates are not connected. A DPG span is of the same design, except the deck is placed on the top of the plate girders, so the entire span is below the track.

A through truss bridge is one of the oldest types of modern bridges. It consists of a series of beams to provide support in multiple directions. A through truss has open sides which support the railroad deck, as well as a structural top over the tracks to provide structural stability. Often looking like a spider web, the design is popular because it uses steel efficiently. As freight cars have gotten larger, a number of the through truss spans have been replaced with more modern plate girder spans, or precast concrete spans by the Rock Island and Iowa Northern. Many of these bridge designs will be cited throughout this material. The rails have also been replaced with heavier rails, and steel ties have also been installed on many tracks. In many places, the railroad signal system has also been removed. The Iowa Northern Railway of 2023 looks substantially different than the Chicago, Rock Island & Pacific Railroad of 1980.

Cedar Rapids to Linn
Trackage Rights
Union Pacific Cedar Rapids Industrial Lead

The track from Cedar Rapids to Linn consists of the former Burlington, Cedar Rapids & Northern/Chicago, Rock Island & Pacific, as well as a part of the former Chicago & North Western mainline. The former C&NW mainline is now the Cedar Rapids Industrial Lead, which extends from Otis (Milepost 77.8) to Beverly (Milepost 82.5). Both stations are on the mainline of the Clinton Subdivision of Union Pacific. The industrial lead passes through Cedar Rapids, with an additional extension northward through North Yard to a connection with the Iowa Northern at Linn, Iowa.

In the Cedar Rapids area, Iowa Northern trains can be seen south and west of downtown as they have trackage rights over the Cedar Rapids & Iowa City to their various yards for interchange purposes. However, Iowa Northern employee timetables begin at Cedar Rapids on the former Rock Island mainline.

97.1   CEDAR RAPIDS – This location is at the 6th Avenue grade crossing in downtown Cedar Rapids, Iowa. It is part of the 4th Street Corridor, today part of the Union Pacific Cedar Rapids Industrial Lead. However, it once was where the Rock Island, Milwaukee Road, and the Chicago & North Western ran side-by-side through town. Later, the tracks were consolidated into one track, and today the Cedar Rapids & Iowa City, Canadian National, and Iowa Northern all use this track for interchange business, as well as the current track owner – Union Pacific.

The National Register of Historic Places Multiple Property Documentation Form for the Industrial Development of Cedar Rapids, Iowa, c. 1865-1965, dated August 2015, is an excellent reference for the railroad and industrial history of Cedar Rapids. It states that "Four major railroad lines passed through Cedar Rapids. The Chicago, Iowa and Nebraska Railroad (1859) eventually became part of the Chicago and North Western Railway (Northwestern/CNW). The Cedar Rapids and St. Paul Railroad (1865) and the Cedar Rapids and Burlington Railway (1866) consolidated in 1868 as the Burlington, Cedar Rapids and Northern Railway. lt became part of the Chicago, Rock Island and Pacific Railway (Rock Island) in 1903. The Dubuque and Southwestern Railroad (1865) was sold to the Chicago, Milwaukee and St. Paul Railroad (Milwaukee) in 1878. The Illinois Central Railroad (1886) was the last major rail line to connect to Cedar Rapids."

This is the south end of the Cedar Rapids Subdivision of the Iowa Northern Railway. As their employee timetable states, Cedar Rapids is a junction location with Union Pacific (UP), Canadian National (CN), and the Cedar Rapids & Iowa City (CIC). To serve the CIC, the Iowa Northern employee timetable states that "IANR trains and engines will use the CIC Main Track between the Jct. switch at Seventh Avenue and the CIC Yard." This interchange is often conducted in the yard near the CIC's shop locations, or even their Smith-Dows Yard on the southwest side of town.

Further north, interchange between the IANR and CN is conducted in either CN "A" or "B" Yard, to the east past the Cargill facility. These yards are accessed by a switch located under the A Avenue Viaduct on the north side of downtown Cedar Rapids. Interchange with Union Pacific generally takes place in the UP North Yard, the former Rock Island Cedar Rapids Yard, at the north end of town past the Quaker Oats facility.

The 4th Street Corridor stretches between Ninth Avenue SE and the CN switch at First Avenue SE. The speed limit on this route is 5 miles per hour. At Ninth Avenue, once known by the Rock Island as CNW Crossing (Milepost 97.0), the Union Pacific (former CNW) route curves east towards Otis, crossing the former CRIP mainline. As stated, the CIC enters the route at Seventh Avenue.

To the east between Fourth and Third Avenues is Greene Park. The park is named for George Greene, who was a lawyer, justice of the Iowa Supreme Court, businessman, philanthropist, and one of the founders of Cedar Rapids. Greene was a major railroad entrepreneur, helping to build numerous railroads across the Midwest, including the Burlington, Cedar Rapids & Minnesota Railroad, which later became the Burlington, Cedar Rapids & Northern Railroad. His Cedar Rapids law firm also represented the Chicago & North Western Railroad.

Look for the grade crossing with Third Avenue SE. Two blocks to the southwest was once the headquarters of the Iowa Northern Railway, in the old Paramount Theatre building. Immediately to the east is the Cedar Rapids Museum of Art with its Grant Wood collection.

Cedar Rapids Union Station

Between Third and Fifth avenues once stood the Cedar Rapids Union Depot, originally built and operated by the Chicago & North Western and the Burlington, Cedar Rapids & Northern railroads. The original station, known as Union Depot, was located on the southwest corner of First Avenue SE and Fourth Street SE, a building described as "a small, unattractive building that hardly suited a growing city." By 1891, an effort began to have a new station built. A report in *The Gazette* newspaper of Cedar Rapids covered the subject with an interview of a CNW official. "The time is coming when Cedar Rapids will have the finest union depot on the line of the Northwestern between Chicago and Omaha, and one of which the people will be proud. Cedar Rapids is growing rapidly now and we have just simply been waiting until we could put up a building that would meet all requirements and demands, no matter how large the city might grow."

In March 1896, land was acquired between Third and Fifth avenues on the west side of the tracks. The two railroads spent $225,000 to build the new 40-foot by 400-foot Union Station, with additional wings on each end. The station opened with a large public gala on January 27, 1897, and soon almost 100 trains a day used the station. The building was constructed of brick and Bedford limestone, with a copper-trimmed tile roof. The most prominent part of the station was a 102-foot central tower, which featured a six-foot diameter clock, and later large C&NW RY and CRI&P RY signs.

Cedar Rapids Union Station had almost every service anyone would need. *The Gazette* of Cedar Rapids described it as such:

> *Architecturally it is all that could be asked for, and adds much to the beauty of the Parlor City. It is built of the finest pressed brick, trimmed with cut stone and adorned with gargoyles that are works of art. It is nearly 600 feet in length, equipped with splendid constructed trainsheds, and its exterior view is pleasing to the eye. The interior is provided with apartments for the various departments which will make their home there; with ticket and baggage rooms, complete in every particular and very commodious; with waiting rooms, large, light and cheery, elegantly furnished with toilets and other necessary appurtenances. Travelers also will have an opportunity to secure their lunches in the station, and smokers also will find special accommodations.*

At the north end was a large restaurant, and then the main waiting room with ticket offices to the east. Further south were rooms for baggage, newspaper shipments, mail, U.S. Express, and American Express shipments. Three tracks served the station, one on the station platform and then one on each side of a covered shed.

Over the decades, the Rock Island and CNW were the only two railroads to use the Cedar Rapids Union Station. In the 1920s, the Milwaukee Road had their station, also used by the Illinois Central, on the southeast corner of First Street. The two interurban railroads, the Cedar Rapids & Iowa City and Waterloo, Cedar Falls & Northern also had their own shared station, located two blocks west of Union Station on Second Street.

Efforts began in the late 1950s to replace the station with a smaller structure and to use the land for parking. As a part of the plan, most of the tracks through town would be removed, Fourth Avenue would be extended through the station site and across the tracks, and both the Rock Island and CNW would move to new stations. Union Station was sold to the city in 1961 for $315,000 and bids to tear it down were opened June 26, 1961. Demolition began on July 3, and Fourth Avenue opened on December 1, 1961. The Rock Island opened a new 30 by 180 foot passenger station at 500 Fourth Street NE, at the south end of their Cedar Rapids Yard, on July 1, 1961. CNW passenger service to downtown Cedar Rapids had ended by this time.

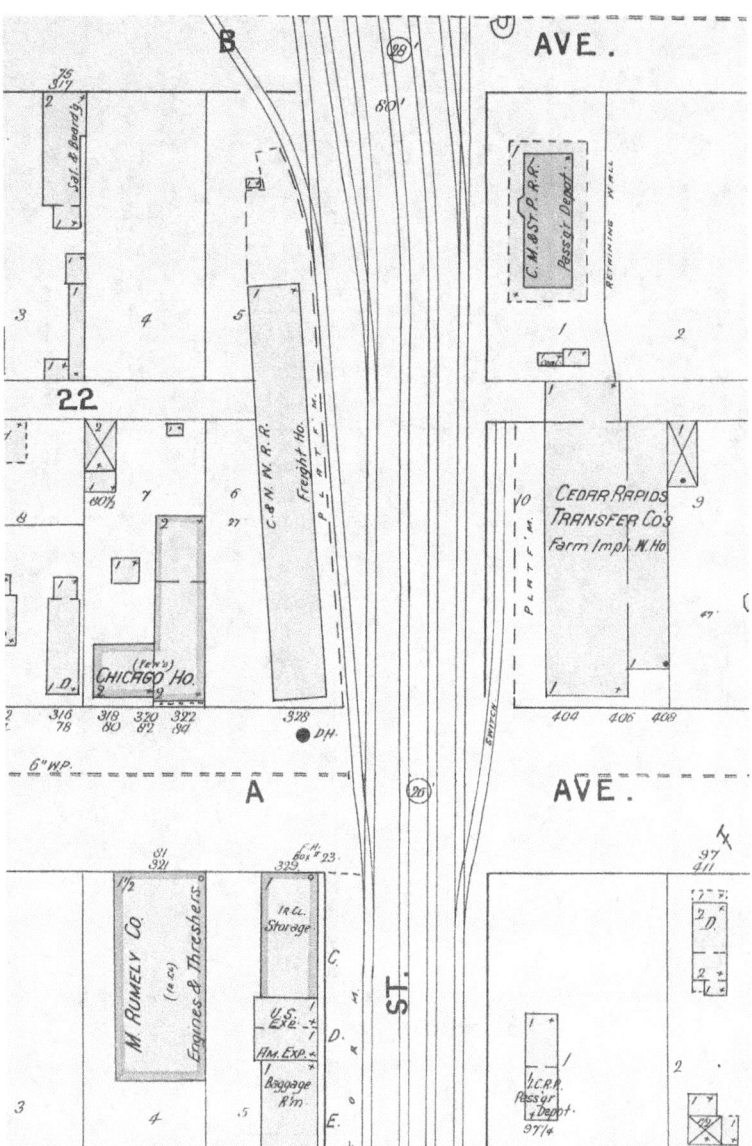

The original Cedar Rapids Union Depot was once on the southwest corner of First Avenue NE and Fourth Street NE, where a hotel now stands. *Sanborn Fire Insurance Map from Cedar Rapids, Linn County, Iowa.* Sanborn Map Company, 1895. Map. Retrieved from the Library of Congress, https://www.loc.gov/item/sanborn02597_003/.

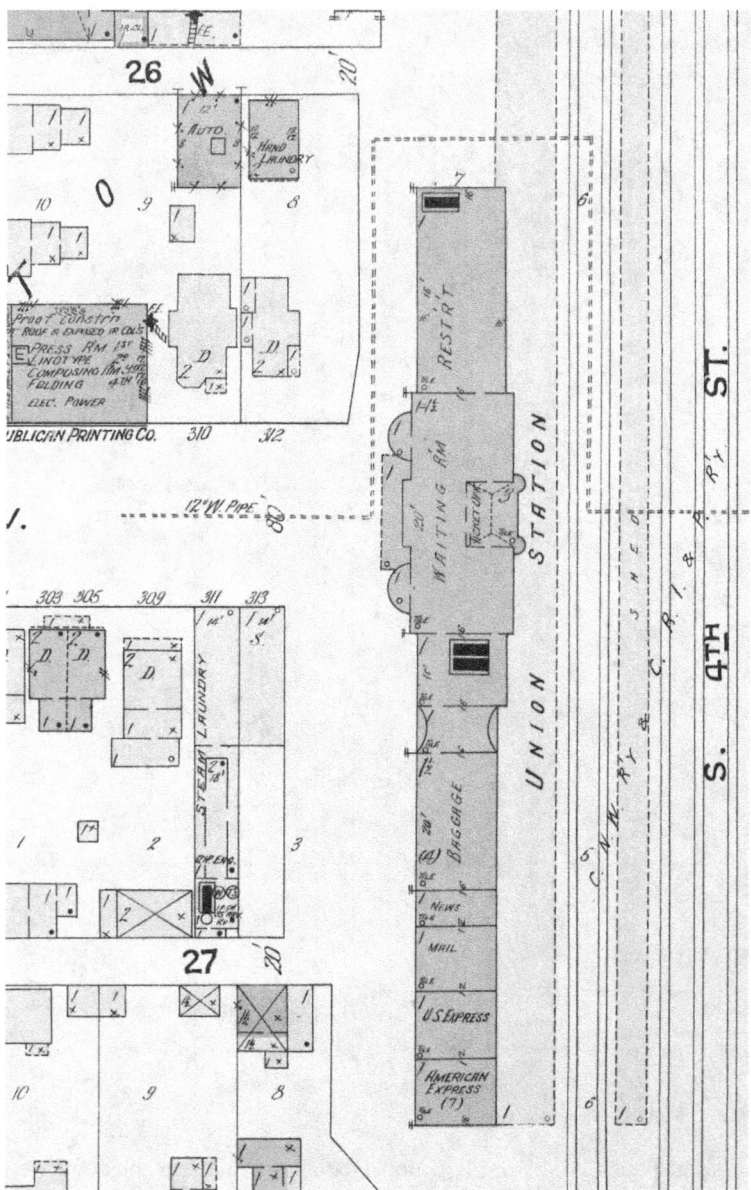

This 1913 map from Sanborn shows the Cedar Rapids Union Station, used by the Rock Island and Chicago & North Western from 1897 until 1961. *Sanborn Fire Insurance Map from Cedar Rapids, Linn County, Iowa.* Sanborn Map Company, 1913. Map. Retrieved from the Library of Congress, https://www.loc.gov/item/sanborn02597_004/.

Burlington, Cedar Rapids & Northern Business Office

Immediately to the east of the tracks at the First Avenue NE grade crossing is the former Burlington, Cedar Rapids & Northern business office. This building was originally built as a three-story Romanesque Revival style headquarters building in 1885. It was designed by the Iowa architectural firm Josselyn and Taylor, which designed a number of area buildings into the 1920s. A fourth floor was added in 1898. Today, the building is known as the First Avenue Building or Pullman Lofts, and the facade has been altered. However, look for the BCR&NRy lettering at the top of this large red brick building.

The parking lot that is now between the BCR&N building and the tracks was once the location of the Chicago, Milwaukee & St. Paul Railway Station, also used by Illinois Central. The Illinois Central paid $104.77 a month, plus 2.5 percent of any betterments for the use of the Milwaukee Road station. The expenses of the station were paid on a wheelage basis.

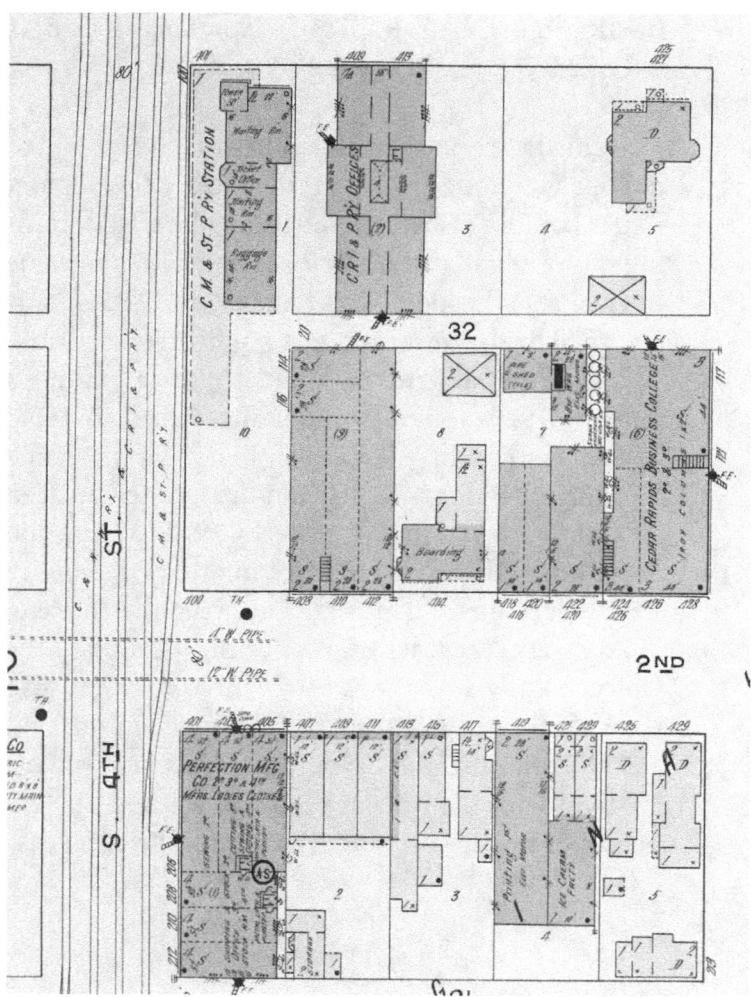

In 1913, Sanborn showed the location of the Chicago, Milwaukee & St. Paul Railway Station as located immediately to the west of the Burlington, Cedar Rapids & Northern business office in Cedar Rapids. *Sanborn Fire Insurance Map from Cedar Rapids, Linn County, Iowa.* Sanborn Map Company, 1913. Map. Retrieved from the Library of Congress, https://www.loc.gov/item/sanborn02597_004/.

The Burlington, Cedar Rapids & Northern business office still stands in Cedar Rapids, and as this photo shows, it is still lettered for the railroad.

City of Cedar Rapids

When Cedar Rapids was first established in 1838 (the year that Osgood Shepherd, the first permanent settler, arrived), William Stone named the town Columbus. In 1841, it was resurveyed and renamed by N. B. Brown and his associates. They named the town Cedar Rapids for the rapids in the Cedar River at the site. Cedar Rapids was incorporated on January 15, 1849.

During the 1850s, Cedar Rapids worked to obtain a railroad, and it was successful. The first rail line was built through Cedar Rapids in 1859, and made the town a major commercial hub in eastern Iowa. The T. M. Sinclair Company, started in 1871 at Cedar Rapids, was one of the five largest packing houses in the world within its first ten years of operation. Cedar Rapids is still home to the largest cereal mill in the world, Quaker Oats, begun in Cedar Rapids in 1873. In the 1920s, Collins Radio Company was founded by local resident Arthur Collins at a time when radio was cutting edge technology. Expanding into avionics and other technologies, Rockwell Collins was acquired by United Technologies Corporation on November 27, 2018, and is now Collins Aerospace. Reportedly, Cedar Rapids currently has more engineers per capita than any other city in the United States.

Over the years, Cedar Rapids has been home to many familiar names in American history. Orville and Wilbur Wright were Cedar Rapids residents from 1878-1881. A little girl named Mamie Doud lived in Cedar Rapids early in the 1900s; she later became First Lady Mamie Eisenhower. Cedar Rapids was the longtime home of artist Grant Wood and his most famous work, *American Gothic*, was painted here. Austin Palmer developed a nationally well-known form of penmanship writing in Cedar Rapids. Recent local residents have included such people as golfer Zach Johnson and actors Ashton Kutcher and Elijah Wood. Some longtime locals call themselves "Bunnies" based upon the way some folks pronounce the town's name: "see der rabbits." Today, Cedar Rapids is the second largest city in Iowa.

When Cedar Rapids became the county seat of Linn County, the city began development of its unique Municipal Island in the historic center of the city, along the Cedar River. This scenic spot became a problem when during the Iowa Flood of 2008, the Cedar River surpassed the 500-year flood plain and placed an estimated 1300 city blocks, or 9 square miles, on both banks of the river under water. Nearly 4000 homes were evacuated and more than 300 destroyed. The Cedar River reached a record high of 31.2 feet on June 14, 2008. Additionally, several rail lines and bridges were washed away by the waters.

The Order of Railroad Telegraphers of North America (ORT) was formally founded during June 1886 at Cedar Rapids. The meeting was organized by Ambrose D. Thurston, who at the time was the publisher of the trade journal *Railroad Telegrapher*. Based in nearby Vinton, Iowa, Thurston started the order as a fraternal organization for telegraphers who had worked for a railroad. This was shown by the organization's constitution which forbade members to strike except in extreme conditions. Also unique was that women telegraphers could be members from the founding of the organization, and some even served as union officials. By 1887, there were more than 2000 members, and more than 9000 members by 1889. The ORT eventually became more active in contract negotiations, eventually sponsoring strikes and pushing for laws that limited the hours that telegraphers were forced to work. In 1965, the ORT changed its name to the Transportation Communications Employees Union. It merged with the Brotherhood of Railway Clerks in 1969.

Another reminder of the railroad history of Cedar Rapids remains to the northwest of downtown. In Usher's Ferry Village is the old Milwaukee Road wooden depot, relocated from Olin, Iowa, a small town to the east. The depot was damaged during the 2008 flooding, but it still stands with a short stretch of railroad track.

97.5 INTERSTATE 380 – The railroad passes under I-380, also known as U.S. Highway 218 and the Avenue of the Saints corridor. The Interstate is less than

75 miles long, with the south end at Interstate 80 at Coralville, Iowa. The north end is at Waterloo, Iowa. Construction took place 1973-1985.

To the north of I-380 is the large Quaker Oats facility, a noted landmark at Cedar Rapids.

This view from July 1941 shows a northbound Rock Island train passing the Quaker Oats elevators at Cedar Rapids, Iowa. This area always seemed to be busy with the tracks of several railroads passing the complex. Vachon, John, 1914-1975, photographer. *Elevators at Quaker Oats plant.* Cedar Rapids, Iowa. July 1941. Photograph. Retrieved from the Library of Congress, https://www.loc.gov/item/2017746578/. (https://www.loc.gov/resource/fsa.8a32868/)

This view from September 1941 shows that the Rock Island handled switching at Cedar Rapids with both steam and diesel locomotives. Wolcott, Marion Post, photographer. *Untitled photo, possibly related to: Grain elevators and flour mill, freight yards.* Cedar Rapids, Iowa. September 1941. Photograph. Retrieved from the Library of Congress, https://www.loc.gov/item/2017824115/. (https://www.loc.gov/resource/fsa.8c28116/)

97.7   IC JUNCTION – This is the junction with the former Illinois Central line that comes in from the Chicago-Omaha mainline at Manchester, Iowa. Today operated by the Canadian National, the junction leads to the former Illinois Central trackage (north side of the power plant), and also the remains of the former Milwaukee Road (south side of the power plant) and on to the Ralston Foods facility to the east.

In 1961, the Rock Island built a new passenger station in this area. It was a lightly colored, single-story structure, typical of the era. The fancy red brick building at this location is not the station, but a nice modern building honoring the area's railroad heritage. To the east is the modern Canadian National office.

98.1   UP NORTH YARD – Known as the Cedar Rapids Yard by the Rock Island, this yard is now used by UP to serve local customers. There are normally several locals based out of this yard, which has almost twenty tracks. Additionally, the Canadian National and both local shortline railroads interchange cars with Union Pacific here. Little else remains of this once major Rock Island terminal.

The *National Register* report on Cedar Rapids stated that the "Burlington, Cedar Rapids and Northern Railway (later the Chicago, Rock Island and Pacific Railway) acquired a large tract of land, north of E Avenue NE, between the Cedar River and Cedar Lake for use as machine shops. The complex contained round houses, sand and coal tipples, engine and car shops, an ice house, spur lines for moving cars to and from the site, and Y-tracks. The railroad shops employed hundreds of workers, many of whom lived in neighborhoods on the west side of the river. The complex remained in use until the 1970s. The site has been cleared and is partially surrounded by a section of the Cedar River Recreational Trail."

Cedar Rapids was CRIP telegraph code "EH" (from *List of Officers, Station Agents, etc. #58*, dated February 1, 1910). During the 1950s, the Rock Island showed this as a yard with a capacity of 3042 rail cars.

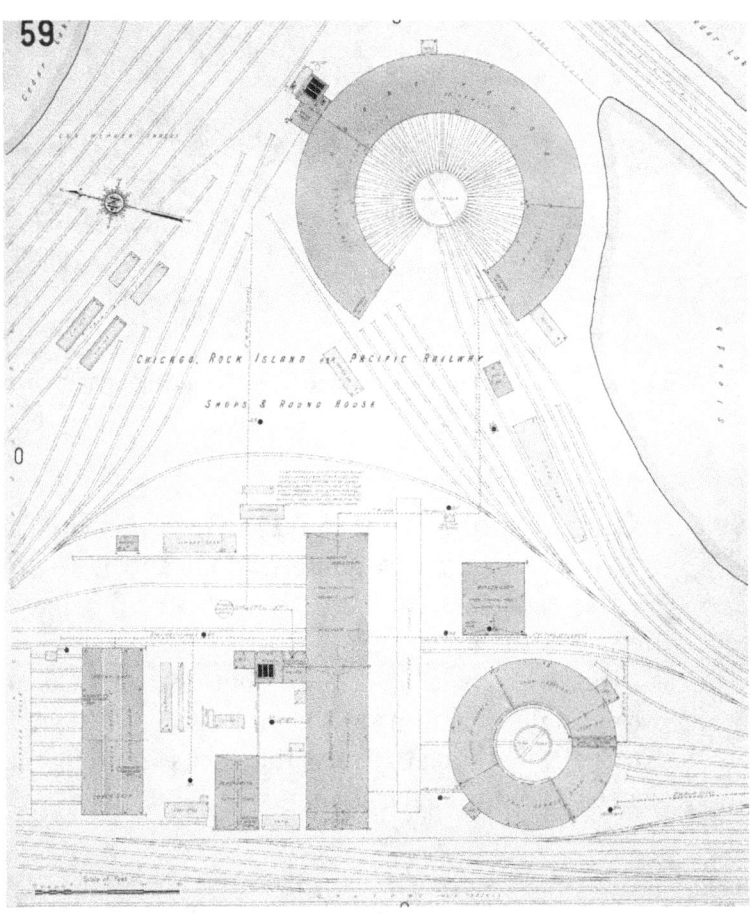

Cedar Rapids Yard once featured a large locomotive and freight car shop complex, located to the east of the mainline. In 1913, this included a 49-stall roundhouse that had replaced an earlier and smaller roundhouse. A machine shop and coach shop were also located here. Sanborn Fire Insurance Map from Cedar Rapids, Linn County, Iowa. Sanborn Map Company, 1913. Map. Retrieved from the Library of Congress, https://www.loc.gov/item/sanborn02597_004/.

The Rock Island Railroad roundhouse no longer stands, but as shown here, parts of it still stood in 1997.

99.6   NORTH YARD NORTH SWITCH – This switch is often cited in radio communications and is where anything going north out of the yard hits the mainline.

The switch is located to the southeast of a Cedar River public boat ramp at what is known as Mohawk City Park. Through this area, the tracks are along the east bank of the Cedar River.

100.6 EDGEWOOD ROAD – This road bridges across the railroad and the adjacent Cedar River, connecting neighborhoods on the higher hillsides on each side of the river.

100.9 LINN – Linn is an Iowa Northern timetable station ("LN") to mark the property line between them and Union Pacific. All track south of this location is owned by UP, and their timetable and rules apply to this track, but Iowa Northern has rights to operate on into Cedar Rapids for interchange purposes. Yard limits also start here for trains heading south. To the west is the Cedar River.

Just west of Linn, the Rock Island curved north-wards using a six-degree curve that is almost 2000 feet long, one of the sharpest curves on the entire line. The railroad followed a small stream to cut the corner of a large bend of the Cedar River.

Linn to Waterloo
Cedar Rapids Subdivision

100.9 LINN – Linn is an Iowa Northern timetable station ("LN") to mark the property line between them and Union Pacific. All track south of this location is owned by UP, and their timetable and rules apply to this track, but Iowa Northern has rights to operate on into Cedar Rapids for interchange purposes. Yard limits also start here for trains heading south. To the west is the Cedar River.

Just west of Linn, the Rock Island curved northwards using a six-degree curve that is almost 2000 feet long, one of the sharpest curves on the entire line. The railroad followed a small stream to cut the corner of a large bend of the Cedar River.

101.7 LINN JUNCTION – This was CRIP station code "JN". It was shown as Linn until the early 1950s, and had a 58-car siding. By the end of the 1950s, it was Linn Junction and no siding was reported.

The Burlington, Cedar Rapids & Minnesota Railway Company built a branch from Linn Junction northward through Independence to Oelwein and on to Postville, Iowa (94 miles), on the Milwaukee Road, by late 1873. This route was later known as the Postville Branch. In 1884, a branch was built from near the north end of the line (Postville Junction) to the northwest to another junction with the Milwaukee Road at Decorah, Iowa. The Postville Branch was abandoned in September 1976. Only a bit of the grade can be seen today at this location.

102.6 BRIDGE ABUTMENTS – On both sides of the tracks are old cement and stone abutments from the former Chicago, Milwaukee, St. Paul & Pacific Railroad (Milwaukee Road, CMSTP&P, or MILW) line between Marion (to the east) and Elberon (to the west). This line became the Milwaukee Road's main route between Omaha and Chicago, used by Union Pacific passenger trains starting in late 1955. It was abandoned in 1980 as a part of the massive Milwaukee Road company reorganization in the late 1970s.

The railroad started as the Sabula, Ackley & Dakota Rail Road, incorporated under Iowa law on June 25, 1870. By the end of 1872, the railroad had reached Marion, just to the northeast of Cedar Rapids. On July 2, 1872, the Sabula, Ackley & Dakota was sold to the Milwaukee & St. Paul Railway Company, which changed the focus of the railroad some. The Milwaukee & St. Paul became the Chicago, Milwaukee & St. Paul Railway Company on February 11, 1874. Financial problems caused by the Panic of 1873, and the need for spending elsewhere on the system, slowed construction across Iowa.

The railroad west of Marion, requiring the abutments and the one-time bridge above, came about when the Chicago, Milwaukee & St. Paul concentrated on building west to Omaha. In 1882, approximately 260 miles of track was built from Marion to Council Bluffs. By 1884, the railroad was hauling 25% of the freight between Chicago and Council Bluffs. Eventually, the railroad obtained trackage rights across Union Pacific's Missouri River bridge, reaching Omaha.

The Chicago to Omaha route was for many years a major route, but one that seemed to be out of place for the railroad. The move in 1955 to handle Union

Pacific's passenger trains was an effort to obtain more freight business. This passenger service ended on May 2, 1971, with the creation of Amtrak, and the last freight train left Marion on March 1, 1980. The track was soon removed.

The Iowa Northern tracks crest just south of these abutments with grades downward toward Cedar Rapids at 1.04% and downward toward the Cedar River at 1.15%.

103.1 CEDAR RIVER BRIDGE – This bridge is made up of five through plate girder spans, a deck plate girder span, some timber spans, and a series of concrete ballast deck spans. The through plate girder (TPG) spans were built in 1905, and the deck plate girder (DPG) span was added in 1960 as the river channel moved. In 1970, a train derailed and took out a sixth through plate girder span on the north end of the bridge, which was replaced by a timber trestle. These spans were damaged during the 2008 floods of the Cedar River and replaced. In 2014, the timber on the north end was replaced with 205 feet of precast concrete ballast deck spans. From north to south, there are then three 88-foot TPGs, two 100-foot TPGs, a 45-foot-long DPG, and then 167 feet of timber trestle on the south end of the bridge. This means that the Cedar River Bridge, also once known as Rock Island Bridge #1031, is 908 feet long. Because of the older design, the bridge has always been noted for its close clearance on the sides of the through plate girder spans.

The Cedar River was named for the large number of red cedar trees that grew along its banks. It has a history of flooding, and has taken out the track north of the bridge several times. The soft grade in the area has led to several derailments. The concrete spans were installed to open up more area for water flow, and to improve the bridge. As a part of the 2014 work, the stone pier for the original through plate girder span was finally removed.

Northward, grades stiffen to 1.20% for about a mile. Starting a few miles north of here, the Iowa Northern installed almost 25 miles of 115# welded rail in 2007-2008. This is a part of a massive track maintenance and engineering program that the Iowa Northern has been conducting over the entire railroad.

The south end of the bridge is surrounded by the Rock Island Botanical State Preserve while the north end is surrounded by the Hanging Bog State Preserve. The Rock Island Preserve is described as a 20-acre site consisting of rare native prairie, wetlands and woodland habitat that is home to over 300 species of native plants. Hanging Bog was deeded to the Nature Conservancy by Leslie F. Clarke in 1968 and was dedicated as a biological State Preserve in 1981. Hanging Bog gets its name from a series of saturated terraces on the lower slopes of the wooded hillsides and is considered to be important for the survival of skunk cabbage, a rare plant that thrives here.

Look to the south and you can see the former abutments of the Milwaukee Road mainline bridge. To the north is the new IA-100 highway bridge, part of the new highway around the west side of Cedar Rapids.

107.3 PALO – Palo was named for the Battle of Palo Alto (1846). Palo Alto, located near today's Brownsville, Texas, was the first major battle of the Mexican-American War. The battle, fought on May 8,

1846, started when 3700 Mexican troops attacked Fort Texas and the surrounding area. General Zachary Taylor responded with 2300 United States troops, pushing the Mexican forces back south.

John Hollenbeck is given credit as being the first settler at Palo. He operated a tavern out of his house, and opened the Palo post office there in 1848. It should be noted that some sources state that Marion resident Dr. Bardwell actually opened a regional post office using the name Palo in 1849. Hollenbeck reportedly served as the postmaster for almost the entire time until his death in 1877. A town grew up around Hollenbeck's house, and it was surveyed on June 10, 1854, formally establishing the community. The community of Palo, located to the east, was incorporated on April 25, 1905. It was never more than a rural farming town, but its population in the 2020 census was 1407, the highest ever recorded. Several new housing subdivisions have certainly helped to more than double the population over the past 20 years.

The Pleasant Ridge Cemetery in Palo is considered to be an unlucky and strange location. First, the cemetery is reached by climbing thirteen steps, certainly an unlucky number. Next, visitors have reported a phantom dog on the steps, balls of green light dancing on gravestones, and a ghost house that sometimes materializes in an adjacent grassy clearing.

Coming from the south, Palo is the location of the Palo Storage Track, 3711-feet long, to the east of the mainline between Chain Bridge Road and the Dry Creek Bridge (three 50-foot through plate girder spans at Milepost 107.2). The small town of Palo, just upstream from Cedar Rapids, is the home of Iowa's only nuclear power plant. A 4-mile-long industrial lead to the Duane Arnold Energy Center breaks off just north of the Dry Creek Bridge. According to the United States Nuclear Regulatory Commission, the Duane Arnold Energy Center (DAEC) is a 1912 megawatt boiling water reactor that began operation in 1974. DAEC had stated its intention to permanently cease power operations in October 2020, but the reactor permanently shut down on August 10, 2020, when a derecho (a land-based hurricane) damaged non-safety related portions of the plant, including the cooling towers.

In 1953, the Rock Island reported that there was a 75-car siding and other tracks with a capacity of 20 cars here. In 1974, the Rock Island showed that the siding at Palo was 3615 feet long, and that there were 763 feet of other tracks and a company telephone available. The Rock Island used "A" for the station code of Palo, but the Iowa Northern uses "LO" for this timetable station.

109.2 COUNTY LINE – Look for the Benton-Linn Road crossing at this location. It is logically the county line between **Linn County** (to the east, or railroad south) and **Benton County** (to the west). The history of **Linn County** dates back to September 20, 1832, when General Winfield Scott and Governor Reynolds of Illinois negotiated a treaty with the Sac, Fox, and Winnebago Indians. This transaction, known as the Black Hawk Purchase, involved 6,000,000 acres of land on the west side of the Mississippi. This purchase did not include all of what is now Linn County, but five years later the United States bought 1,250,000 more acres immediately west of the first tract, also from the Indians. This strip was twenty-five miles wide and its western boundary was nearly identical to the existing western boundary of Linn County.

The first settlers arrived in the area in 1836 and 1837. Soon after, the Iowa Territory was created by an Act of Congress (on June 12, 1838). Linn County was organized by the first legislative assembly of the Iowa Territory on January 15, 1839, with the act providing that the County of Linn be organized from and after June 10, 1839. Linn County was named after Lewis Fields Linn (1795-1843), a senator from Missouri. Linn was a champion of the Western territories, and several midwestern and western states have a county named in honor of the senator.

A site was selected for its first county seat along Indian Creek, and was named Marion, after the Revolutionary War general Francis Marion. As early as 1855, there were debates over moving the county seat to the fast-growing Cedar Rapids, southwest of Marion, but it was not until November 6, 1919, that there were enough votes in favor of the move. Cedar Rapids deeded a portion of Mays Island to the county as a site for the new courthouse. Today, with more than 230,000 residents, Linn County is the second most populous county in the state of Iowa.

Benton County was formed on December 21, 1837, from sections of Dubuque County. It was named after U.S. Senator Thomas Hart Benton of Missouri. Benton fought in the War of 1812 and was a noted attorney. Vinton is the county seat. Even though the first mention of Benton County was in 1837, the first white settlers didn't arrive until early in 1839, when several families named Wright, Smith, Scott, and Lockhart settled in different parts of the county.

With the beginning of white settlements in the area, the boundaries of Benton County had to be more clearly defined. Because of that, Section 9 of an Act of the Territorial Legislature of Iowa, entitled "An act to establish new counties and define their boundaries in the late cession from the Sac and Fox Indians, and for other purposes," approved February 17, 1843, provided "That the following boundaries shall constitute a new county and be called Benton..."

The population of Benton County was 25,575 in the 2020 census. This is pretty typical for the county, which has had a population between 20,000 and 25,000 since the 1870 census. The change has been that the residents once mostly worked on farms, while today many travel to Cedar Rapids for employment.

109.5 BEAR CREEK BRIDGE –Bear Creek starts northwest of Shellsburg with the merger of Oppossum Creek and Wildcat Creek. It flows to the southeast and then into the Cedar River several miles to the east of here. Because of the easy grade through the rolling terrain, the railroad follows Bear Creek northward into Shellsburg. To cross Bear Creek, the railroad uses a single span deck plate girder bridge.

111.2 BEAR CREEK BRIDGE – This 6-span deck plate girder bridge is supported by limestone block piers. The 240-foot bridge was built by the American Bridge Company of New York. Three spans date from 1902, while three others date from 1959. The west end of the piers show that the line was once double track at this location.

This bridge over Bear Creek at Milepost 111.2 shows that the railroad here once consisted of two tracks.

111.4 SHELLSBURG – While there are no side tracks here today, Shellsburg is a timetable station for the Iowa Northern. The Shellsburg Elevator is located here. The elevator is owned by West Side Unlimited. The company was founded by the Vogt family in the 1960s to salvage grain spills at train yards. Today, the company provides grain storage, cleanup of spills, grain transportation, and other similar services.

Shellsburg was established in June 1854 with 24 lots and two streets – Main and Pearl. One of the first settlers was John Sells. There are several versions of how the town was named. One states that Sells wanted to name it after himself, but others had problems with that, so a similar name was chosen. Another version states that the town was actually named for Schellsburg, Pennsylvania, the home of one of those that laid out the town.

A post office opened here on November 24, 1856, and the town was a stop on the Cedar Rapids and Vinton stage line. The stage was replaced in December 1869 when the first passenger train arrived. Shellsburg was incorporated on February 19, 1874, and today's population is about 1000.

Like most towns along the Iowa Northern Railway, there is a large grain elevator alongside the tracks at Shellsburg. Here, Iowa Northern #461 is shown passing the elevator on a summer day in 2012.

The Railroad and Its Customers

While there are no side tracks or sidings at Shellsburg today, the Rock Island served several customers here during the 1910s. The railroad had their depot on the north side of the tracks, located west of Railroad Avenue, now Sells Street. Across the tracks was the Shellsburg Grain & Lumber Company. They had a 12,000-bushel elevator that was built in 1903. It was powered by a gasoline engine. There were stock pens east of Railroad Avenue in the same area. A siding and a house track both were located south of the mainline. Several sawmills and a flour mill were also nearby.

Just west (railroad-north) of the siding was a spur track that served the Iowa Canning Company, located south of the mainline. Further west and also to the south was the Shellsburg Brick & Tile Company. This company was founded by Samuel Shannon about 1865 and manufactured common brick and drain tile. During the late 1800s, Shellsburg was considered to be a major center for the production of brick and tile. Its brick was used in a number of area buildings, including the Rock Island station at nearby Vinton. The brick business was also helped locally when Shellsburg enacted a city ordinance in 1914 requiring buildings in the business district to be fireproof.

Into the 1950s, the Rock Island had a 52-car siding here as well as 22 car lengths of other tracks. At the time, Shellsburg was also a train order station. In 1974, the railroad had 1100 feet of "other tracks" at Shellsburg, plus a company telephone. Shellsburg has historically carried the station code of "SG", and the IANR still uses that as its code.

111.5 BEAR CREEK BRIDGE – The railroad uses a 6-span, deck plate girder bridge to make this Bear Creek crossing possible. This bridge is 240 feet long, and consists of 2 spans built in 1897, 3 spans built in 1901, and 1 span built in 1903. The spans were built by the American Bridge Company of New York and the Lassig Bridge & Iron Works of Chicago.

Heading north, the railroad climbs a short grade of 1.18%.

114.2 BEAR CREEK BRIDGE – Oppossum Creek and Wildcat Creek merge to form Bear Creek just upstream of this bridge, which consists of two 60-foot deck plate girder spans. Just to the north, the railroad passes through a two-span, 90-foot-long through plate girder bridge over Oppossum Creek.

115.6 GREASERS – Greasers, spelled Gressers in several sources, was listed in early Rock Island timetables, but was not assigned a station code in the *1910 List of Officers and Station Agents.* There was a 53-car siding at Greasers into the 1960s. Look for the 28th Avenue road crossing and the old grade to the east.

Philip Greaser arrived in Benton County and purchased a claim on May 16, 1851. He had previously been a native of Hesse-Darmstadt, Germany. His August 4, 1914, obituary stated that he donated $200 and the right-of-way across his farm to the Cedar Rapids & St. Paul to "insure the first and only railroad built into Vinton."

119.6 MUD CREEK BRIDGE – Mud Creek forms about ten miles to the southwest and flows into the Cedar River less than a mile to the east. The railroad uses a large stone arch span to cross Mud Creek and a local road. Not far north of here is the south switch of the Vinton Siding.

For southbound trains, there is 6600 feet of steady 0.8% grade that starts in Vinton and ends about Milepost 119. It climbs from 811 feet at Vinton to

863 feet. This part of Iowa features a number of low rolling ridges that the railroad had to climb.

120.4 VINTON – Look for the sign calling Vinton the "City of Lights". The community of Vinton began its history known as Northport in the mid-1800s. The first post office in Benton County was established here on October 1, 1846, and was called Vinton. The name Vinton came from a member of Congress from Ohio who encouraged towns to carry his name. The man was Samuel Finley Vinton (1792-1862), member of the United States House of Representatives from Ohio. He was noted for his service on the Public Lands Committee, and in 1862 was appointed by President Abraham Lincoln to appraise the value of slaves freed in the District of Columbia. He had experience with railroads, having served as president of the Cleveland & Toledo Railroad.

Initially an outpost for trading, Vinton quickly became a support center for the burgeoning number of farmers who were taking advantage of the rich soil around the town. John Tilford became a key person in the development of Vinton as he purchased and then sold home lots from downtown south toward the current fairgrounds. For both business and community interest reasons, Tilford donated many of his tracts to churches and other community resources.

The people of Vinton had worked to obtain a railroad for many years. When the Cedar Rapids & St. Paul Company promised to build a road through Benton County by way of Vinton for the sum of $75,000, and the further donation of the county's swamp lands, worth some $15,000 more, the community had their wishes fulfilled. The first train arrived at Vinton on December 12, 1869, and the occasion was celebrated by a banquet at the Asylum on the 21st. Because of the industry brought by the railroad, the town grew to a population of roughly 3500 by the early 1900s.

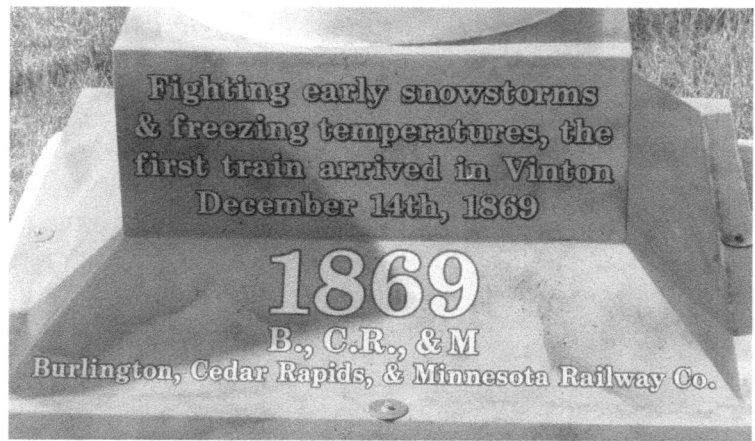

This monument to the construction of the Burlington, Cedar Rapids & Minnesota Railway stands near the depot at Vinton, Iowa.

Vinton has traditionally been a farm-based community with a number of small businesses. However, by the late 1970s several key businesses had shut their doors including Hawk Bilt, Perfex and Iowa Ham. The decade of the 1980s saw continued change as Vinton went from five implement dealers to one, the Chevrolet dealership closed its doors and the remaining small factories closed as well. Interstate 380 was completed in 1985 and changed the traffic flow through Vinton overnight. With U.S. Highway 218 no longer the primary thoroughfare between Cedar Rapids and Waterloo, businesses that relied on the traffic struggled, with many closing. Efforts were made to fight these economic issues, including Vinton Cruise, Party in the Park, and the "Wall Dogs" celebration resulted in eye-catching and appealing murals on downtown buildings. Vinton reached its peak population in 2010 with 5257 residents, but was back down to 4938 in the 2020 census.

The Railroad at Vinton

In 1885, the railroad was lined with a series of businesses, and had a passenger station and freight house on the north side of the tracks at the Wallace Street grade crossing. Nearby were shippers like the A. S. Chadbourne Elevator & Feed Mill, R. H. Reed Elevator & Feed Mill, the Mitchell & Company butter and egg packing warehouse, and W. A. McAllister grain warehouse. An issue with the location is that the streets of Vinton have been renamed, with numbered streets running east-west and numbered avenues running north-south. A few avenues on the west side of town use letters of the alphabet.

By 1892, the Kelly Canning Company was located to the north between the grade crossings of Dustin Street (later Fourth Avenue) and Benton Street (later Fifth Avenue) and had a capacity of 70,000 cans in ten hours. In 1899, plans were already underway to build a new passenger station closer to downtown between Main (later Second Avenue) and Taylor (later Third Avenue). By this time, the railroad right-of-way and the lots along it had become more formalized, with the tracks occupying what was shown as Railroad Street, later Seventh Street, although it has never been used as a city street.

The new passenger station was located on the north side of the tracks and centered on Taylor Street (later Third Avenue). The old passenger station was now shown to be the freight office, stock pens were located at the east end of town along Jay Street (later

Tenth Avenue), and Kelly Canning was now known as the Iowa Canning Company, shown to have a capacity of 150,000 cans per ten-hour day. By the early 1910s, the street names had been changed. Some of the businesses had changed names, but grain, feed and canning still dominated the businesses along the tracks through Vinton. Throughout this time, the railroad consisted of two tracks through town, with a number of spur tracks into the industries. The mainline was to the north while a siding was to the south. A set of crossovers to the east of the new station connected the two tracks. Heading west (railroad-north), the south track was the main going west to Iowa Falls.

Like most towns in Iowa, the businesses slowly closed, moved away, or began to use trucks to move their products. The Great Depression of the 1930s only accelerated this change. However, Vinton remained important enough to have a train register and order station at the depot, and a 65-car siding plus 167 carlengths of other tracks in 1953. This changed a little over the next two decades as there was an 8130-foot-long siding plus 4922 feet of other tracks in 1974. Vinton was still a train order office, especially because it was a junction station.

East of Sixth Avenue is the start of the Vinton Siding. The siding is to the south and goes several blocks east to a set of crossovers. In this area is Cedar Bend Industrials, a family owned and operated company specializing in custom seed conditioning and packaging. The firm started in the 1970s when Sanders and Sons started cleaning seed, and today has expanded to clean and condition soybeans, corn, cereal grains and grasses, removing stems, pods, rocks, dirt, and other foreign material prior to planting or processing. While the company primarily ships by truck, it does advertise the ability to ship on the Iowa Northern Railway. The siding continues eastward and is shown by the Iowa Northern to have a storage capacity of 5583 feet. There is only one track through Vinton now and the junction to the former Iowa Falls Branch can be found at A Avenue.

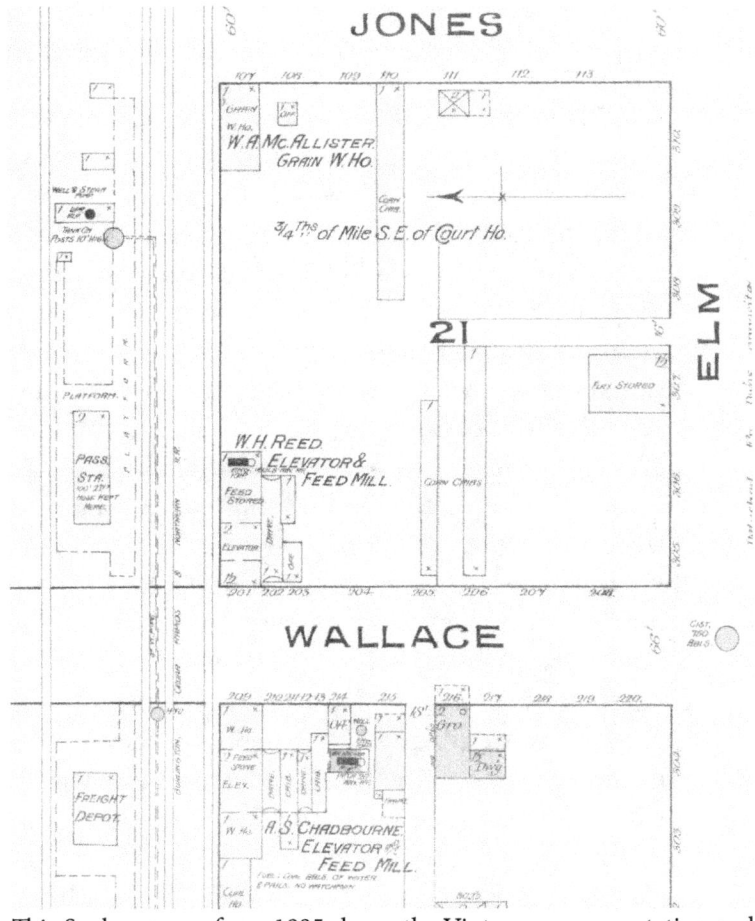

This Sanborn map from 1885 shows the Vinton passenger station and freight depot of the Burlington, Cedar Rapids & Northern, *Sanborn Fire Insurance Map from Vinton, Benton County, Iowa.* Sanborn Map Company, October 1885. Map. Retrieved from the Library of Congress, https://www.loc.gov/item/sanborn02857_001/.

Vinton Depot

Located to the north of the tracks (railroad-east) at 612 Second Avenue is the former Rock Island depot, listed on the National Register of Historic Places in 1990. Construction on the brick building began on August 1, 1899, and construction was completed by the building's dedication on March 1, 1900. This was the second station at Vinton, the first was built by the BCR&N on the east side of town.

During the late 1880s, the railroad was making a number of improvements, and decided to move their station closer to downtown Vinton. By early 1889, the railroad had reached an agreement with the city to obtain two blocks of land for less than $500. H. F. White, the railroad's architect and chief engineer, designed a unique brick and limestone station, but one that still resembled others on the line. A. H. Connor & Company of Cedar Rapids built the 132-foot-long and 28-foot-wide station for $40,000.

When completed, the building was a major attraction for the community. The *Cedar Rapids Republican* newspaper stated that the people of Vinton now have "the best depot in Iowa, for the size of the city. Cedar Rapids, Sioux City, Des Moines and a few other cities have larger depots, but even these larger cities do not have any better depots – they simply have larger ones." The building features brick walls with a limestone foundation. The limestone foundations were quarried near Postville (to the northeast) and the brick was fired at nearby Shellsburg. The roof was originally tile. The building featured a men's waiting room with no attached toilets at the west end of the building, with a ladies waiting room with attached toilets to the east. The station offices were located between the two waiting rooms. A baggage and express room was located west of the open archway.

The Rock Island depot at Vinton is now the Vinton Depot Museum, operated by the Benton County Historical Society. From 1967 until 1981, the building housed the offices of the Hawk Bilt Company, a farm equipment manufacturer.

The Vinton station was used to handle passengers, issue train orders, register trains on and off of the Cedar Falls Branch, and as a communications office. Because it served trains on both the mainline and siding, its hours changed based upon the train schedules. In 1953, the communications office was open 7:30am until 3:30pm and 7:00pm until 3:00am, seven days a week.

The railroad operated the station until 1967, using the call letter "N", but the IANR uses "VN". The station later became the sales office for Hawk Bilt farm implements. After Hawk Bilt moved away, the building became the property of the Benton County Historical Society, which restored much of the structure and opened up a museum that tells the history of Vinton, the railroad, and Hawk Bilt. Adjacent to the station is former CRIP caboose #17023.

Rock Island caboose #17023 is on display next to the depot at Vinton.

After the station closed, the railroad opened a small metal office building which still stands at 8th Avenue. Across the mainline is the Vinton Storage Track. Located to the west (railroad-north) is the Vinton Branch to the Shellsburg Elevator.

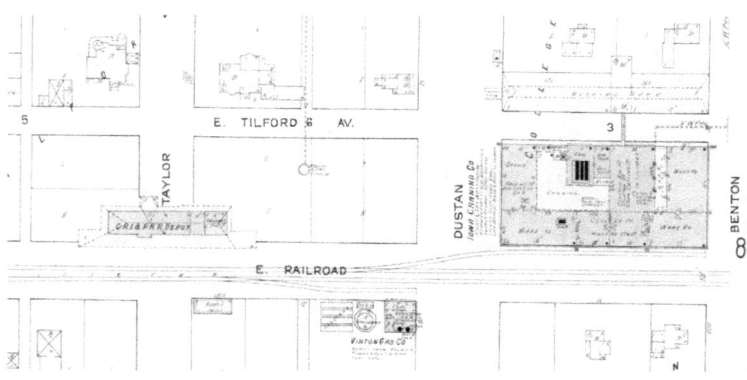

This Sanborn map from 1913 clearly shows the Vinton Depot, built by the railroad and opened on March 1, 1900. *Sanborn Fire Insurance Map from Vinton, Benton County, Iowa*. Sanborn Map Company, September 1913. Map. Retrieved from the Library of Congress, https://www.loc.gov/item/sanborn02857_005/.

121.2 VINTON JUNCTION – The Burlington, Cedar Rapids & Minnesota Railway Company built a branch from Vinton to Dysart, Iowa, (16 miles to the west) via Garrison by the end of 1872. At one time, this line extended on west to a junction of CRIP and Illinois Central lines at Lynch, Iowa, and on to Cedar Falls. In 1966, the line was known as the Cedar Falls Branch, but a few years after it was built, it was known as the Pacific Division and was being built toward Sioux Falls and Watertown, South Dakota. In 1898, it was known as the Sioux Falls Division. A statement at the time was, "In addition to the main line, the Sioux Falls division ends here and all the trains from that division are thrown to the main line at this point, so that Vinton catches all the trains from both main line and branch."

The Iowa Northern still lists Vinton Junction in their timetable, giving it station code "N". In July 1994, IANR abandoned the branch from west of Vinton to Dysart. Part of the line (1.25 miles) remains as a stub track, known as the Dysart Spur Track, to serve the Tama-Benton Cooperative complex. The Tama Benton Cooperative was formed in 1912 and often used the name Tama Benton Grain Company. The name comes from Tama and Benton counties where it handles grain storage and marketing. The firm has elevators at Vinton, Dysart, and Clutier.

Past the Tama Benton Cooperative elevator the line to Dysart is gone, replaced by the Old Creamery Trail. However, some new track has been built and curves to the south to serve the Vinton facility of New Century FS. As stated by the company, FS companies are located in the Midwest and northeastern United States and in Ontario, Canada. This plant offers seed, fertilizer, chemicals, custom spraying, crop scouting, top dress urea, and hot loading chemicals. For the Iowa Northern, the station Vinton (DS) is defined as Tama Benton Cooperative and New Century FS.

122.0 HINKLE CREEK BRIDGE – Hinkle Creek flows eastward into the Cedar River. It forms about 15 miles to the west near Garrison. The bridge consists of two 60-foot deck plate girder spans, installed here in 1966.

122.3 TERRA AND USS SPURS – Heading north out of Vinton, there are two spur tracks to the east that once served the facilities of Terra and U.S. Steel.

124.9 BRIDGE - This is a 70-foot-long, five span timber pile trestle. It crosses a small stream that drains the fields to the southwest.

125.1 PRATT CREEK BRIDGE – This 84-foot-long deck plate girder bridge was built in 1899 and has been scheduled by the Iowa Northern for replacement. The bridge crosses Pratt Creek as it flows into the Cedar River, leading older Rock Island records to show that the bridge crossed the Cedar River. Pratt Creek forms in farmland about a dozen miles to the northwest.

The railroad is at an elevation of 791 feet. Heading north, it begins to climb and ends with 4800 feet of 1.06% grade at Milepost 129. The elevation there is 870 feet.

128.9 MOUNT AUBURN – This area was known as Big Hill by the Indians and known originally as Mount by the first settlers. A post office opened in the area in 1865 using the name Mount Auburn, apparently named after Mt. Auburn, Illinois. As a community grew, settlers Milton S. Hall, Sarah A. Hall, Thomas D. Lewis, and Mary A. Lewis organized the town on June 19, 1871, not long after the railroad arrived. To help local farmers, a cheese factory was started in 1873, producing 27,484 pounds of cheese the next year. The community incorporated on November 19, 1906.

Mount Auburn is at the peak of the hill, with grades of almost 1.2% downward in both directions. The siding at Mount Auburn was laid in June 1870. A railroad turntable, used to turn locomotives when Mount Auburn was the end of track, was later taken out and moved to La Porte. Mr. Soesbe was the first Station Master and the first merchant, and Mr. Gudgel built the first grain warehouse, providing the railroad many carloads of business.

Mount Auburn was known as station "AU" by the Rock Island when its depot was located south of Third Street on the west side of the mainline. During the early 1900s, there was a siding to the west that looped around the station and served the St. Clair & Son elevator to the south of the depot. The elevator was built in 1898 and had a capacity of 20,000 bushels. South of the elevator was a set of stock pens at a hog meat processing plant.

During the 1950s, Mount Auburn had a 53-car siding. The industry tracks had a capacity of 16 freight cars. Today, Mount Auburn is known as "MT" by the Iowa Northern. The Mount Auburn Elevator Track is on the west side of the mainline. In 2020, Mount Auburn had a population of 162. It is a small town with a grain elevator and post office surrounded by miles of farmland.

130.2 SPRING CREEK BRIDGE – From here, Spring Creek flows northward into the Cedar River. Spring Creek starts on a small hill about seven miles to the southwest. This hillside must be somewhat wet as maps show that seven different streams start here. The railroad bridge is a 55-foot deck plate girder span

132.8 COUNTY LINE – Look for the road crossing with Main Road. To the south is **Benton County** while to the north is **Black Hawk County**.

Black Hawk County was created in 1843 and named for the Sac war leader who lost the war that bears his name (and who never set foot in the area named for him). However, with no permanent population, the county was first administered by Delaware County (1843-1845), then Benton County (1845-1851), and then Buchanan County (1851-1853). In 1853, Black Hawk County was allowed to organize its own government and elect officers, making Waterloo its county seat.

Meanwhile, in 1845, at a ford in the river that had long been used by Indian tribes, settlers George and Mary Hanna created the community of Prairie Rapids that attracted other settlers. At about the same time, a mill was built nearby at what was called Sturgis Falls. Thus Sturgis Falls and Prairie Rapids, later to be renamed Cedar Falls and Waterloo, became in 1845 the first settlements in Black Hawk County, and between them at the end of the year they boasted the county's entire white population of thirteen pioneers.

Surrounded by some of the richest farmland to be found anywhere on the globe, the cities of Black Hawk County became important centers for the agricultural community. Despite a brief period of high water, which allowed the steamboat *Black Hawk* to make twenty-four round trips between Cedar Rapids and Waterloo in 1859, the Cedar River was not destined to provide a transportation advantage. Thus, it was the arrival of railroads that opened up the nation's markets to the farms of Black Hawk County.

Today, Black Hawk County is Iowa's fifth-most populous county, with 131,144 residents reported in the 2020 census.

133.1 ROCK CREEK BRIDGE – This stream forms on the northwest side of Dysart and flows northeast to here and then on to the Cedar River. This bridge consists of four 35-foot-long deck plate girder spans.

135.2 LA PORTE CITY – Dr. Jesse Wasson, founder of the town, named it after his old hometown in Indiana. The "City" part of the town's name came about when it was discovered that there was already a La Porte in Iowa. The town and post office were established on July 16, 1855, using the name Laporte City. By the 1860s, the town bragged of a grist mill and sawmill on Big Creek, now known as Wolf Creek, and the first iron bridge built in Black Hawk County, built across Big Creek in 1867. In 1870, an election was held to incorporate the community, and the vote was 110 for incorporation and 75 votes against. Laporte City was officially incorporated on February 11, 1871, and it had a population of 1006 in its first census in 1880.

By the late 1880s, Carver & Husman had a horse-powered grain elevator south of the BCR&N, which was located on the northwest corner of the

Cedar Street grade crossing. At the time, the railroad had three tracks, including the mainline, east of the depot and one long house track to the west.

In 1910, maps show that the Iowa Canning Company was served by a rail spur running down Railroad Street to the east of the mainline near the station. There were now two elevators south of the depot, one operated by a Mr. Skinner, and the other by the W. A. Bryant & Son's Grain Company. In 1911, the Rock Island built a new depot several blocks to the north at Maple Street. Within a few years, the grain elevators merged and became the Farmer's Cooperative Union grain elevators, with the railroad stock pens across the tracks to the east.

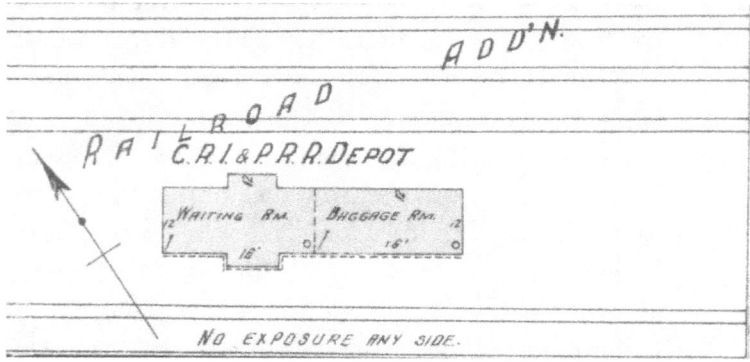

In 1913, Sanborn included this drawing of the new Rock Island's depot in the company's maps of La Porte. *Sanborn Fire Insurance Map from La Porte City, Black Hawk County, Iowa.* Sanborn Map Company, October 1913. Map. Retrieved from the Library of Congress, https://www.loc.gov/item/sanborn02707_003/.

For years, Rock Island Railroad passengers boarded and disembarked from trains at this depot in La Porte City. In 2010, a tamper was parked next to the depot after a busy day of track work.

The year 1912 saw much excitement at Laporte City as the Waterloo, Cedar Falls & Northern (WCF&N) interurban system built through the city as part of its plan to build on south to Cedar Rapids, which it reached in September 1914. To reach its new station, which was built on Main Street in downtown Laporte City, the WCF&N installed a wye on their line and built a branch towards town. The WCF&N was located just east of the Rock Island mainline, and the new branch crossed the Rock Island at the Commercial Street grade crossing. The branch continued to Main Street, turned north to the station at Locust, then turned eastward to Third, and then south back to the branch at Commercial. This created a simple one-block loop in Laporte City, providing access to the downtown market. The interurban's brick station is a one-story rectangular building, with dimensions of 54' x 37'. The station was closed in 1928 and a new utilitarian freight depot was erected by the main line. After it was closed, the station was sold to La Porte City, which still uses it as part of the city hall complex, located at 202 Main Street. The building was added to the National Register of Historic Places in 1979.

The depot of the Waterloo, Cedar Falls & Northern also still stands at La Porte City and is now used as the city hall.

By the 1920 census, the population had grown to 1443 and Laporte City was serving the local farms with retail and commercial establishments. What was shown to be the Farmer's Co-operative Exchange had two grain elevators, listed as having capacities of 15,000 and 23,000 bushels. In 1923, the name of the city and post office were both changed to La Porte City, as used today. The Great Depression was hard on La Porte City, and the Iowa Canning plant was sold to the Minnesota Valley Canning Company by the end of World War II.

On June 9, 1925, a large gathering of members of the Order of Railroad Telegraphers took place at La Porte City. On that date, a bronze tablet was installed at the Rock Island depot to honor Ambrose Duane Thurston. "Daddy" Thurston was the founder and first executive of the order, created at La Porte City in 1886. The tablet read: "Ambrose Duane Thurston, while employed as telegrapher in this city, formulated a plan for a permanent organization of his craft, resulting in the establishment of the Order of Railroad Telegraphers, June 9, 1886."

The Order of Railroad Telegraphers wasn't the only railroad organization formed at Laporte City that year. Another one of the significant events was the founding of the Brotherhood of Maintenance of Way Employees. This organization merged with another one operated in the southeast in 1891 to form the International Brotherhood of Railway Track Foremen of America, which became the Brotherhood of Railway Trackmen in 1896. After merging with a similar Canadian organization in 1902, the International Brotherhood of Maintenance of Way Employees was created.

La Porte City had a number of tracks, essential to handle the freight business. There was a 66-car siding, plus 65 car lengths of other tracks. The railroad had a train order station at their depot.

The La Porte City FFA Historical and Ag Museum was founded in 1970 by the La Porte City FFA Chapter. It is located in La Porte City's original historic fire station and jail house on Chestnut Street. This building is listed on the National Register of Historic Places. In 2016, the museum added a restored 1861 log cabin to its collection.

The population of La Porte City peaked at 2324 in the 1980 census and has remained about the same since. Today, La Porte City is still a busy railroad town. The 3300-foot-long East Elevator Track and the Fertilizer Track are to the east and the 1592-foot-long Elevator Track is to the west. The elevator complex has continued to go through a change of ownership. It was used by the East Central Iowa Co-operative, a part of the Cenex operation. Today, it is shown to be the Mid-Iowa Cooperative, acquired in 1996 through a series of mergers. The history of the farmer-owned Mid-Iowa Cooperative dates back to April 25, 1907, and now includes 1400 members. It claims to be the largest direct-ship farm-to-market grain procurement company in the Midwest, and it handles a full line of Purina feed products, ranging from cattle, swine and other animal feed including cat and dog food. The company also operates a fleet of trucks and has a major role in the new Shell Rock Soybean Processing Plant.

The former Rock Island brick depot also still stands at Walnut Street and Maple Street, next to a city park. The station used the code of "PA", the same as the Iowa Northern uses today in their timetable. The WCF&N right-of-way through this area is used by the Cedar Valley Nature Trail. The Cedar Valley Nature Trail is one of the pioneer "linear parks" in Iowa, built on the abandoned WCF&N railroad right-of-way in the early 1980s. The trail is 52 miles long and passes through four counties. Fran Allison of *Kukla, Fran & Ollie* fame was a resident of La Porte City. While the city is a regional farm community, its population was only 2284 in the 2020 census.

135.6 WOLF CREEK BRIDGE – Wolf Creek is a fairly large stream with a large watershed. It is listed as a major tributary of the Cedar River. It starts about 70 miles west of here near Grundy Center. The stream was once known as Big Creek and a grist mill and sawmill were located on it in the 1850s through 1870s. La Porte City still sits in Big Creek Township, named for the stream. The railroad crosses

Wolf Creek using an 80-foot through plate girder span that is listed as having close clearance between trains and the bridge structure. There is also 118 feet of trestle on its north end.

To the east of the Iowa Northern's bridge is a bridge on the WCF&N right-of-way. Through this area, the WCF&N right-of-way is used by the Cedar Valley Nature Trail. The Cedar Valley Nature Trail is one of the pioneer "linear parks" in Iowa. The trail was built in the early 1980s and is 52 miles long, passing through four counties.

To the north of La Porte City and to the east of the tracks at Milepost 136.7 is the Brett Klima Wildlife Area, marked by signs and a small parking lot. The habitat found in the park consists of lowland prairie and flood plain woodlands. Most of the acreage is open to public hunting. The 100 acres near the park entrance has undergone a three-year prairie restoration project in partnership with the local chapter of Pheasants Forever.

138.5 MUD CREEK BRIDGE – This stream is crossed by the railroad on two 60-foot deck plate girder spans. Mud Creek forms in several fields only about a mile or two to the west, and flows east into the Cedar River after another five winding miles.

141.3 MILLER CREEK BRIDGE – This stream forms from a series of small springs on the rolling hills about ten miles to the southwest. It collects a number of other similar small streams before passing under the tracks. The railroad bridge consists of three 35-foot-long deck plate girder spans, all set on concrete piers. Several miles to the east, Miller Creek flows into the Cedar River. Much of the creek's route to the east is through the Cedar River Natural Resource Area.

143.3 WASHBURN – The first town in this area was Gilbertville, platted in 1856 several miles to the east. The town was created by John Chambaud and John Felton of Dubuque, who thought that the Illinois Central would build through the area. They planned to build a flour mill nearby on the Cedar River. Chambaud and Felton promoted the town around the world, and many early settlers were French, earning the town the nickname of French Town. The town soon had a brewery, tannery, flour and lumber mills and a French-language newspaper. However, when the railroad built to the north and the town didn't grow further, there were charges of fraud against the developers.

However, when the Burlington, Cedar Rapids & Minnesota Railway Company built through this area in 1871, a number of area residents moved close to this railroad. Washburn was platted on March 13, 1880, by the Close (Jonathan and Sarah) and Mead (Joseph and Sarah) families, but named for Levi Washburn, an area farmer. The town was able to initially grow due to the BCR&M/BCR&N railroad tracks. The population reached 79 in 1902, and then 94 in 1925. A map from 1910 showed that there was a siding through town to the west of the mainline, plus an industrial siding to the east that served a number of industries. The industries included, from north to south, a coal yard, grain elevator, two lumber sheds, stockyard, and corn crib. The stockyard was apparently a busy place as the Village Grove Stock Farm was just northwest of town while the Washburn Stock Farm was to the northeast.

When platted, most of the town was designed to be north of Main Street, today's Washburn Road, the only major grade crossing in town. However, today's Washburn has moved to the south. The depot was between the mainline and the industrial siding just south of Main Street. "UN" was the station code used by the Rock Island for Washburn. Today, the Iowa Northern uses "WB". Legend has it that a worker helping to build the railroad died while working here and he was buried under the tracks.

During the 1950s, there was a siding with a capacity of 75 cars. Other tracks had a capacity of 32 freight cars. The 1265-foot-long Washburn Elevator Track is now to the east, serving the Heartland Co-op facility. In 1987, three cooperatives merged to create Heartland Co-op. The three cooperatives were Panora Farmers Cooperative, formed in 1947; Farmers Cooperative Company, formed in 1919 at Dallas Center; and Minburn Cooperative, created in 1945, and expanded by buying a plant at Granger in 1986. Over the next few years, several more elevators were bought. In 1993, a newer Heartland Co-op was created by the merger of Alleman Cooperative Company, Mitchellville Cooperative, the former Avon Grain Company facilities, and the original Heartland Cooperative. The cooperative has continued to grow across the region by merging and buying other elevators and cooperatives. This facility was once the privately owned Washburn Elevator, later acquired by Central Counties Cooperative in 2005 and eventually becoming part of Heartland. The facility has 1,976,000 bushels of grain storage capacity.

Today, Washburn is an unincorporated town with approximately 1000 residents (870 in the 2020 census). Heading north from Washburn, the railroad starts passing through light industry and new housing subdivisions created as Waterloo continues to grow.

145.7 EAST SHAULIS ROAD – While it doesn't look it from the railroad, Shaulis Road is a major road in south Waterloo. To the west are a number of tourist and recreational facilities, including theme parks, waterparks, and golf courses. To the east, the road heads to scattered housing and the Cedar Valley Nature Trail.

At the East Shaulis Road grade crossing is a large yellow "Y" sign. This is the beginning of yard limits for northbound trains as they enter Waterloo. There is also an automatic equipment identification (AEI) reader system here. AEI is the system that uses tags on freight cars, along with radio frequency trackside readers, to track the movement of railroad equipment. With Waterloo having multiple routes and multiple interchange possibilities, tracking the freight cars as they enter and exit the Waterloo Yard is an important process for the Iowa Northern.

147.1 INTERSTATE 380 – The railroad passes under I-380, also known as U.S. Highway 20, Iowa Highway 27, and the Avenue of the Saints corridor. The Interstate is less than 75 miles long, with the south end at Interstate 80 at Coralville, Iowa. The north end is at Waterloo, Iowa. Construction took place 1973-1985.

147.8 SOUTH SWITCH OF BRYANT YARD – This is often a busy location as trains switch the yard, and trains to and from Cedar Rapids leave and enter the yard. Immediately to the east is the large Aspro asphalt facility. This plant started as the Waterloo Dredging Company asphalt plant, and a sand and gravel deposit. In 1973, Aspro was created to buy the property. Today, Aspro operates two Waterloo asphalt plants and does asphalt paving, general road and street construction, and commercial parking lot construction.

148.2 BRYANT YARD – This location used the name East Yard and Bryant during Rock Island days. Bryant Yard is the name used today. The Rock Island showed that East Yard had a capacity of 243 freight cars, and the siding had a capacity of 95 freight cars. The Iowa Northern states that "Bryant Yard is a mechanical and engineering facility in Waterloo, but also has a 15 car self-serve transload track and a cross dock to handle boxcar transloading." During the mid-1980s, U.S. Highway 218 was relocated and expanded through Waterloo. Unfortunately (maybe fortunately), IANR's Waterloo Yard was in the way and government funds were used to build a new yard and shop near southeast Waterloo, called Bryant Yard ("BY"). The yard, located to the east of the mainline, has six yard tracks plus a two-track locomotive shop, a two-track maintenance-of-way shop, a fuel track, plus several other facilities. For example, Iowa Northern also serves transload customers at Bryant Yard. This facility has cross dock operations for direct truck-to-rail transload currently handling feed ingredients, dust control, industrial and food grade starches, and boxcar commodities. A Waterloo Switcher is based here. Much of the railroad's track and bridge engineering work is also based here.

Bryant Yard at Waterloo is the home of the railroad's locomotive shop, shown here with several locomotives parked outside.

The north end of Bryant Yard is essentially at Mitchell Avenue, Milepost 148.6. A "granite & brick works" and a "cement works" were served here by the Rock Island in 1910. Further north where the La Porte Road grade crossing is now, the Rock Island once had a spur track to the east to serve a paper mill located on the Cedar River.

150.2 CNW CROSSING – The Iowa Northern tracks begin to turn east here to connect with Union Pacific. At one time, the Rock Island tracks went straight and there was a diamond between the Rock Island and the Chicago & North Western (earlier Chicago Great Western) at this location. In 1974, the Rock Island employee timetable showed this crossing to be an automatic interlocking.

150.3 WATERLOO – Milepost 150.3 marks the change of ownership between the Iowa Northern and Union Pacific's former CNW/CGW line through town. It is also the north end of the Cedar Rapids Subdivision.

As mentioned with the Bryant Yard description, during the mid-1980s, U.S. Highway 218 was changed in Waterloo and tracks were moved or abandoned. The former Rock Island mainline between Waterloo and neighboring Cedar Falls was removed, and IANR secured trackage rights over what can only be called a convoluted route between the two cities. Heading north, Iowa Northern trains swing to the east and begin about a mile of trackage rights over Union Pacific (former CNW/CGW) tracks that include a bridge over the Cedar River. Near Linden Yard, Iowa Northern trains enter Canadian National (once interurban line Waterloo, Cedar Falls & Northern) tracks and circle around the north side of Waterloo. At West Waterloo Tower, IANR trains head west on CN's (ex-IC's) Chicago-Omaha mainline, again cross the Cedar River, and hop back on Iowa Northern tracks at Cedar Falls Junction.

The beautiful CRIP brick and stone passenger station still stands at 333 West 4th Street and Bluff Street, several blocks north of where the IANR curves to join with Union Pacific. In Rock Island days, it was assigned station code "WA" while the freight house was "WF". The station was built in 1890 and was originally known as the Burlington, Cedar Rapids & Northern Railway Passenger Depot. It later became the Rock Island Passenger Depot. To the south was once the BCR&N freight house, used as the baggage room by the mid-1910s. There were a number of tracks to the west of the BCR&N Passenger Depot. The two eastern tracks belonged to the Rock Island while the two western tracks were the property of the Chicago Great Western. Even after passenger service ended during the 1960s, the railroad continued to use the station for freight and billing purposes for a few more years. It was then sold and renovated by Heaton, Adams & Company. Today, the building is labeled with the name Adams Everson & Company.

During the 1950s, downtown Waterloo was shown to also host a rail yard, generally used to serve local industries. The yard had a capacity of 375 freight cars. The station was also used as a register station.

The former Rock Island station at Waterloo still stands, but the main-line tracks that once passed by the station have been removed.

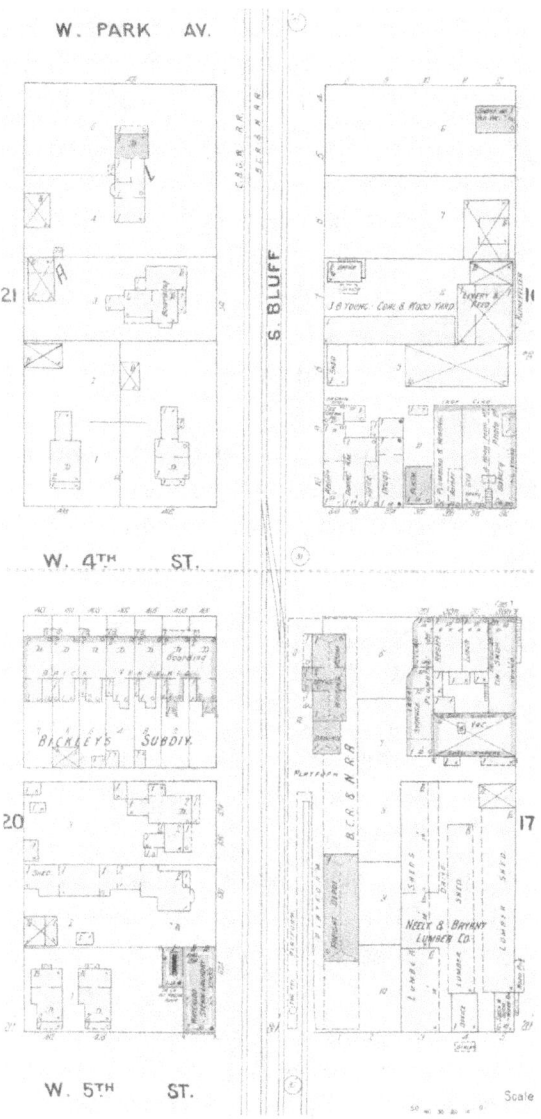

The Burlington, Cedar Rapids & Northern Railway Passenger Depot still stands in Waterloo at the intersection of today's Washington and West Fourth streets. Built in 1890, it was used by the Rock Island Railroad into the 1960s. The building still stands, renovated for other uses. *Sanborn Fire Insurance Map from Waterloo, Black Hawk County, Iowa.* Sanborn Map Company, September 1900. Map. Retrieved from the Library of Congress, https://www.loc.gov/item/sanborn02862_004/.

Today, the Iowa Northern uses a code of "WD" for Waterloo. Also in town is the old Chicago Great Western freight house, located at East 6th Street and 800 Sycamore and listed on the National Register of Historic Places. The former CGW passenger station at 2nd Street at Bluff is long gone, with the site under today's U.S. Highway 218. The downtown passenger station on 6th Street was torn down in 1973. If you are looking for other interesting Waterloo railroad structures, you can also check out the old Illinois Central two-story yard office and roundhouse off East 4th Street. The former IC train station was along the east shore of the river at the end of Park Street, where the railroad had a number of facilities, all now gone.

Waterloo History

Waterloo and nearby Cedar Falls have a long history of fighting to be the major city in Black Hawk County, and in this part of Iowa. In 1845, Sturgis Falls (Cedar Falls) and Prairie Rapids (Waterloo) were the first settlements in Black Hawk County and hosted the county's entire white population of thirteen pioneers. When the Iowa legislature created a commission to locate the county seat, the two communities competed heavily until a vote selected the more centrally-located Waterloo in 1855. However, it was the railroad industry that actually made the biggest impact when the first railroad (Dubuque & Sioux City Railroad, later Illinois Central) arrived in the area in 1861, reaching Waterloo first. This trend continued in 1870 when the Illinois Central Railroad chose Waterloo over Cedar Falls as the site of its repair shop. Meanwhile, in 1876, the Iowa

State Normal School (today's University of Northern Iowa), a teacher's college, opened with twenty-seven students in a former orphanage in Cedar Falls. Because of these factors, Cedar Falls gained the nickname of "The Lawn City", in sharp contrast with Waterloo which by the early 1900s was known as "The Factory City".

Even in Waterloo, there was division as the Cedar River passes through the middle of the city. Residents of Waterloo clashed on the location of the courthouse. Separate school districts existed until 1942. Probably the most famous divide came about in 1898 when philanthropist Andrew Carnegie began his campaign to subsidize the building of public libraries. Of the 1679 libraries built by the program's end in 1919, 101 were built in Iowa, with two being built in Waterloo. To settle the peace, Carnegie increased his donation from $30,000 to $40,000 to allow two smaller libraries to be built instead of one large library. Two small, but tasteful, buildings were finally erected after two years of negotiations to settle the argument between residents of the east and west side of the river. They were known as the East Carnegie Library and the West Carnegie Library. Both opened about 1906, and the west library building is now used by a law firm while the east library building now houses city offices.

Because of the railroad transportation available, Waterloo has long been an industrial community. For example, John Deere has several factories (tractors, engines, etc.) in Waterloo. This started in 1918 when Deere acquired the Waterloo Gasoline Engine Company in order to add the popular Waterloo Boy tractor to its other successful farm implement lines. Another major employer was the Rath Packing

Plant, one of the largest meat packers in the nation in its time (Rath closed in 1985). Both companies were heavily unionized in 1942, making Waterloo known as a strong "union town" ever since. Additionally, the prominence of agriculture in the region led to the Dairy Cattle Congress settling permanently in Waterloo in 1912 and, as the National Dairy Cattle Congress, becoming one of the nation's premier livestock shows.

On the negative side, in 1968, the manager of a Kentucky Fried Chicken restaurant in Waterloo was convicted of sexually assaulting a minor and was given an 18-month sentence. He later got in a great deal more trouble. His name? How about John Wayne Gacy! (For those who don't know, between 1972 and 1978, Gacy raped and murdered at least 33 young men and boys in the Chicago area. Although some of his victims' bodies were found in the Des Plaines River, he buried 26 of them in the small crawl space underneath the basement of his home.)

On the other hand, a more patriotic story is also based here. Waterloo was the home of the Sullivan brothers. George, Francis, Joseph, Madison and Albert Sullivan all joined the U.S. Navy shortly after Pearl Harbor and served together on the USS Juneau, a light cruiser. All but George were killed when the ship was sunk during the Battle of Guadalcanal. George died while hanging from a lifeboat several days later awaiting rescue.

While some of the major industries are gone, enough remain that Waterloo has a population of approximately 70,000, making it the eighth-most populous city in Iowa.

Waterloo to Linden Avenue Junction
Trackage Rights
Union Pacific Waterloo Industrial Lead

As previously mentioned, the Iowa Northern uses trackage rights over Union Pacific and Canadian National to travel between Waterloo and Cedar Falls. Heading north, Iowa Northern trains turn east and begin about a mile of trackage rights over Union Pacific (former CNW/CGW) tracks that include a bridge over the Cedar River. Near Linden Yard, Iowa Northern trains turn north and enter Canadian National (once interurban line Waterloo, Cedar Falls & Northern) tracks and circle around the north side of Waterloo. At West Waterloo Tower, IANR trains head west on CN's (ex-IC's) Chicago-Omaha mainline, again cross the Cedar River, and re-enter Iowa Northern tracks at Cedar Falls Junction.

The current Union Pacific tracks were originally the Chicago, St. Paul & Kansas City Railroad (CSP&KC), the third railroad to reach Waterloo. The CSP&KC started as the Minnesota & North Western (M&NW), which built a line south from St. Paul, Minnesota, to Dubuque, Iowa, by 1884. The M&NW was acquired by the CSP&KC in 1887, and the new railroad built lines west to Omaha, Nebraska, south to St. Joseph, Missouri, and east to Chicago, Illinois, by 1890. The construction caused the railroad to fail, and it was reorganized as the Chicago Great Western (CGW) in 1892. During the early 1900s, the railroad continued to face financial difficulties before being acquired by the Chicago & North Western Railway in 1968. Soon, most of the former CGW routes were abandoned. The C&NW was purchased by Union Pacific in April 1995, explaining this isolated piece of Union Pacific track.

324.8 WATERLOO – This is the former CNW milepost for the CNW/CRIP diamond.

325.1 IANR CONNECTION – This is the location of the Iowa Northern-Union Pacific junction shown in the *Union Pacific Iowa Area Timetable #4*, dated October 10, 2011. It is at the west end of the Cedar River bridge.

325.1 CEDAR RIVER BRIDGE – This 730-foot-long, eight-span through plate girder bridge, was built in 1901 by the American Bridge Company of New York. It was partially swept away by high floodwaters on the Cedar River on Tuesday, June 10, 2008. Spans 5 through 8 fell into the river. The issue in rebuilding the bridge was that while Union Pacific owns the bridge, it is the Iowa Northern that uses it. While plans were made to rebuild the bridge, negotiations were conducted to determine where the funds were going to come from, and both railroads waited for the Corps of Engineers to sign off on the design phase. This situation caused big headaches for rail customers across eastern Iowa. Everything from grain to ethanol to John Deere tractors had to be detoured for hundreds of miles. For example, much of the traffic had to go north to Manly – then back south to Nevada – then east to Cedar Rapids, all in Iowa. This was a detour of around 300 miles for nearly two-thirds of the rail company's business. As Dan Sabin, Iowa Northern President, said at the time, "It's tremendously expensive."

During the reconstruction of the bridge, spans 5 through 8 were heat straightened and reinstalled, piers 5-7 were rebuilt, and all new decking and rail was installed. On September 28, 2009, the new bridge was commemorated and the first IANR train crossed it on October 6, 2009.

The Cedar River was named for the large number of red cedar trees that grew along its banks. The Meskwaki, or Fox Indians, called the river the Red Cedar River. It forms in Minnesota and flows 338 miles to the south-southeast to a junction with the Iowa River. At the junction, the Cedar River is actually larger than the Iowa River.

325.3 CHICAGO GREAT WESTERN RAILROAD FREIGHT DEPOT – To the north of the tracks is the University of Northern Iowa Center for Urban Education (UNI-CUE), housed in the former Waterloo freight depot of the Chicago Great Western. This 1903 structure is listed on the National Register of Historic Places (1997), and is described as a two-story concrete block freight depot built on a rough limestone foundation. The building features round arch freight doors and a simple wood cornice. There is also a concrete block addition on the southwest side. This was the second freight house built by the railroad, which was also the first to build a depot downtown.

Illinois Central once had an interchange connection here. The track headed south along the Cedar River, and then looped back east to connect to the mainline. Most of this grade is still visible.

326.0 BRIDGE OVER CANADIAN NATIONAL – This is the Waterloo Subdivision of the Canadian National. It is part of the route from Chicago west to Fort Dodge, where the line splits to reach Council Bluffs and Sioux Falls, both in Iowa. Below is the east end of Canadian National's Waterloo Yard. At the west end of the yard is the old roundhouse and turntable.

326.1 LYNDEN AVENUE JUNCTION – Is it Linden or Lynden? Both spellings have been in print over the years. This location is also known as Waterloo by the railroad. It is a junction between Union Pacific and Canadian National, used by the Iowa Northern as a part of their Waterloo to Cedar Falls route.

Union Pacific's Linden Yard is just east of this location. According to an article in the April 2008 *Railroads Illustrated*, "UP bases a switch crew out of the former CGW yard, in northeast Waterloo, to serve a contingent of customers in the area, like farm tractor and implement manufacturer John Deere; Tyson Foods, formerly Iowa Beef Processors; and Kinder Morgan Terminals, a fertilizer warehouse and distribution center." Linden Yard and a few miles of track to the east are all of the railroad in Waterloo that Union Pacific owns. Therefore, Iowa Northern handles traffic in and out of Waterloo for Union Pacific, mainly from the UP at Cedar Rapids.

Linden Avenue Junction to West Waterloo
Trackage Rights
Canadian National North Waterloo Industrial Track

Much of this line was once the Waterloo, Cedar Falls & Northern Railway, an interurban railroad operating between Waterloo and Cedar Falls. In 1895, the Waterloo & Cedar Falls Rapid Transit Company (W&CFRT) was created to build an electric rail system in the Waterloo-Cedar Falls area. By 1897, a line connected the two towns. With plans to operate throughout Iowa, the company was reorganized in 1904 as the Waterloo, Cedar Falls & Northern Railway (WCF&N). Connecting with the Chicago Great Western allowed the line to also handle carload freight, an important part of the railroad's operation. The WCF&N even operated on the Chicago Great Western using trackage rights.

Besides the grade used as a trail and the few miles of track at Waterloo, car #381 is another reminder of the Waterloo, Cedar Falls & Northern Railway. This car, reportedly the last streetcar to operate in Iowa (August 1, 1958), now operates on the Midwest Electric Railway at Midwest Old Threshers in Mt. Pleasant, Iowa.

In 1912, the WCF&N reached La Porte City, and then Cedar Rapids on September 14, 1914. The route into Cedar Rapids allowed the interurban to interchange traffic with the Milwaukee Road, Chicago & North Western, Rock Island, Illinois Central, and Cedar Rapids & Iowa City. The railroad became known as the "Cedar Valley Road" and operated modern passenger and freight trains using a 1300-volt, D.C. system. The company fell into receivership in 1940 and was reorganized in 1944. The company was able to turn a profit due to freight business during the 1940s, but regular passenger service ended in 1952, with charter and excursion service lasting until 1958.

The Illinois Central and Rock Island railroads bought the WCF&N in 1956, creating the Waterloo Railroad. Electric service ended in 1957 and trains used a fleet of small diesel locomotives. The Rock Island sold its part of the company in 1968, and the IC immediately began abandoning most of the Waterloo Railroad. The trackage around Waterloo was sold to the Chicago, Central & Pacific Railroad in late 1985, then reacquired by IC in 1996. Canadian National bought the IC in 1999. Much of the route south of here is now the Cedar Valley Nature Trail.

2.6 LINDEN AVENUE JUNCTION – Iowa Northern trains enter this former Illinois Central line, once operated by the Waterloo, Cedar Falls & Northern (WCF&N), at this location. Some records show this track to be the North Waterloo Industrial Lead. The route taken from here to get back on the former Rock Island line includes 2.6 miles to West Waterloo via IC's WCF&N, and then 6.0 miles on the former Illinois Central Chicago to Omaha mainline.

There is a short siding north of Albany Street.

1.8 NEWELL STREET – This was once the junction where the Waterloo, Cedar Falls & Northern came in from the southeast.

0.3 WATERLOO, CEDAR FALLS & NORTHERN SHOPS – When the Waterloo, Cedar Falls & Northern was expanded, 23 acres of farmland were acquired here and shops were built for the railroad. The facility included a 12-stall roundhouse with a 55-foot turntable, a machine shop, and several large car sheds. A great article about the Waterloo, Cedar Falls & Northern Railway can be found in the August 24, 1912, issue of *Electric Railway Journal* for those that want to know more.

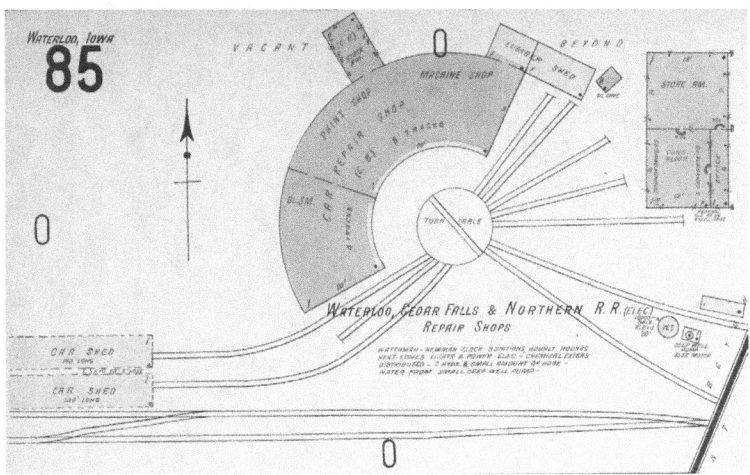

North of the current route around Waterloo was once the shops of the Waterloo, Cedar Falls & Northern. The facility included a 12-stall roundhouse, a machine shop, and several car sheds. *Sanborn Fire Insurance Map from Waterloo, Black Hawk County, Iowa.* Sanborn Map Company, 1918. Map. Retrieved from the Library of Congress, https://www.loc.gov/item/sanborn02862_007/.

0.0 **WEST WATERLOO** – This is the junction with the Chicago-Omaha mainline of the Canadian National, formerly Illinois Central. At one time this place was known as West Tower. When heading towards Cedar Rapids, the Waterloo, Cedar Falls & Northern would cross here, head around the northeast side of Waterloo on the route the Iowa Northern uses, dive under the Chicago Great Western route to Oelwein, and then head south towards La Porte City. The WCF&N had a wye here that allowed trains to also head north to Waverly by following the Illinois Central route to Mona Junction and then directly north.

Just to the north is a large flooded quarry. This facility clearly shows on early maps of the area as the Waterloo Stone Company. A second quarry was just to the east with the name Christian Margayant. Between the two was a large round building identified as the "Quarry Round House" which resembles a typical railroad round house.

West Waterloo to Cedar Falls Junction
Trackage Rights
Canadian National Waterloo Subdivision

This route is the Canadian National mainline west of Chicago to western Iowa. It started as the Dubuque & Pacific Rail Road Company (D&P), incorporated in Iowa on May 19, 1853. After some construction, but with an inability to pay its bills, one of the largest stock holders, Morris K. Jesup, forced its receivership. Jesup then incorporated the Dubuque & Sioux City Railroad (D&SC) on August 13, 1860, and acquired the D&P on August 21, 1860. Jesup then controlled the railroad for twenty-seven years, reaching Cedar Falls in 1861. The Illinois Central, which supported the line in its efforts to grow west out of Chicago, leased the railroad on October 1, 1867. Interstate Commerce Commission records state that the D&SC "has been operated by the Illinois Central continuously since October 1, 1867, with the exception of the period between October 1, 1887, and March 15, 1888."

Over the next few decades, ten other railroads were acquired by the D&SC, giving the railroad more than 760 miles of track in Iowa, Minnesota, and South Dakota. The line eventually disappeared as part of the Illinois Central. The trackage around Waterloo was sold to the Chicago, Central & Pacific Railroad in late 1985, then reacquired by IC in 1996. Canadian National bought the IC in 1999. Today, Canadian National operates this line as their Waterloo Subdivision.

277.5 WEST WATERLOO – This is the milepost used by the Waterloo Subdivision. Here, Iowa Northern trains enter the Canadian National mainline when heading from Waterloo to Cedar Falls.

278.6 SUSIE – This is the west end of doubletrack. A small yard begins on the north side of the mainline. An industrial track heads north from here, serving several shippers in an industrial park. North of the industrial park is the abandoned track of the WCF&N that went north from here to Waverly, Iowa.

281.0 MONA JUNCTION – The railroad that heads north was built as the Cedar Falls & Minnesota Railroad (CF&M), organized in 1858 by several individuals connected to the Illinois Central. By the mid-1860s, the railroad had reached Waverly, Iowa, and in 1867 the railroad was leased by the IC. The CF&M reached Minnesota in 1870. The railroad built north from there as the Albert Lea & Southern Railroad, eventually reaching Albert Lea about 1900. In 1984, the line became the Cedar Valley Railroad, which was sold to the Cedar River Railroad on December 31, 1991. The Cedar River Railroad was owned by the Chicago, Central & Pacific Railroad, which had bought the mainline in late 1985. The line again became part of Illinois Central in 1996, and then Canadian National in 1999. It is now operated as the Osage Subdivision of CN.

The name Mona Junction comes from the town of Mona, Iowa, located just south of the Iowa-Minnesota boarder. Mona was founded in 1869 by the railroad.

281.5 U.S. HIGHWAY 218 – The railroad passes under this elevated four-lane highway just southwest of the Waterloo Regional Airport. Part of the highway started in 1913 when farmers and communities along the route began to build a roadway. Each section was marked by six-inch red balls to help identify the road, and to help keep traffic on the proper route. This gave it the name the Red Ball Route. In 1926, it was designated as U.S. Highway 218 when the original United States highway system was created.

U.S. Highway 218 is 319 miles long and connects Keokuk, Iowa, with Owatonna, Minnesota. It is part of the route of the Avenue of the Saints, which connects St. Louis, Missouri, and Saint Paul, Minnesota.

282.8 CEDAR RIVER BRIDGE – This is a three span Pratt through truss rail bridge over the Cedar River in Cedar Falls, Iowa. Built in 1899 by the American Bridge Works of Chicago, Illinois, it is 444 feet long. The Illinois Central once had a passenger station and a freight house east of the Main Street grade crossing just east of the Cedar River bridge.

At the west end of the bridge is Sturgis Park and the Ice House Museum. Where the park is now was once a mill race lined with mills, powered by water backed up by the dam in the Cedar River. The Ice House Museum is reportedly the only ice harvesting museum in the country using an original ice house. The round building was built in 1921 and can hold 16 million pounds of ice. Nearby are several other historic structures, including a 1909 one-room schoolhouse and the Behrens-Rapp Filling Station. Several blocks to the south is the Victorian Home & Carriage House Museum, which houses the William J. Lenoir Model Railroad Collection. Lenoir was an early modeler of trains, hand making a large layout in the scale of 1/4 inch to the foot (known as O Scale).

During the late 1800s and through much of the 1900s, the Chicago Great Western had a branch-line just south of the mainline of Illinois Central that served several area industries. There was even a connecting track between the two railroads at Clay Street.

283.5 CEDAR FALLS JUNCTION – This is where the Canadian National and Iowa Northern connect. This junction once included a diamond, but today uses switches to make the crossing. The Cedar River is immediately to the north.

Cedar Falls to Manly
Manly Subdivision

As previously discussed, the route from Waterloo north to Plymouth Junction was built in 1872, where construction stopped due to the financial panic in 1873. The Burlington, Cedar Rapids & Minnesota Railway Company defaulted on its bonds during November 1873, and fell into receivership on May 19, 1875. During June 1876, the railroad was sold to the Burlington, Cedar Rapids & Northern Railway Company (BCR&N). With the new ownership, the railroad was extended to Manly Junction by July 5, 1877. As with the line south of Waterloo, it went through several owners until becoming part of the Iowa Northern Railway in July 1984.

The original Rock Island route headed northwest from Waterloo and followed the south side of the Cedar River. It crossed Dry Run and entered Cedar Falls about where the Cedar Falls Utilities power plant was built. As of 2023, there are plans to abandon the trackage through Cedar Falls, including the street trackage down Fifth Street.

155.7 END OF TRACK – This is the end of what is known as the Cedar Falls Spur, the former Rock Island mainline through Cedar Falls south of the junction with Canadian National at Cedar Falls Junction. The track from here south to Waterloo was abandoned during the mid-1980s. The track in this area is often used to temporarily store rail cars for area shippers. The right-of-way immediately south of here is now part of the Riverside Trail.

156.0 CEDAR FALLS UTILITIES (CFU) – This coal-fired electric generating plant was served by the Iowa Northern. About the year 2000, the IANR began delivering coal brought to it by CN in small car blocks from a mine at Galacia, Illinois. About 2005, CFU upgraded their unloading and stockpile facilities to handle 100-car-plus unit trains and in June received a test unit train loaded with low-sulfur coal mined at the Spring Creek Mine in Montana. The routing was interesting with BNSF serving the mine and delivering the train to CN at Sioux City, Iowa. CN then brought the train to IANR at Cedar Falls. Unit trains have also been delivered from other mines with some coming down from the UP at Manly, which brings trains loaded at the Monterey Mine in southern Illinois. The delivery of coal trains ended about 2010, ending the need for the rail line through Cedar Falls except for car storage and occasional transload movements.

156.2 CNW CROSSING – This is the location of the former crossing of the CGW branch into Cedar Falls. Today, the various lines have been combined to create a wye, with the south leg running down Twelfth Street.

To the east is Washington Park, acquired in 1920 thanks to a financial gift from Henry Pfeiffer, which required the park to be named for his brother, Washington Pfeiffer. The park once featured a 9-hole golf course, but it was destroyed during the 2008 floods. Today, the park includes a ball field, shelters, and a boat ramp.

In 2014, the Iowa Northern conducted a track inspection class for many of its maintenance-of-way employees, and they spent time on the tracks near the CFU power plant learning how to stringline track to ensure its geometry compliance with various federal regulations.

156.5 CEDAR FALLS – The former CRIP brick and stone passenger station still stands in Cedar Falls at 422 Main Street, where it has been used as a restaurant, bank and other businesses. Records indicate that the station opened in 1871, and that it has been the scene of at least two presidential speeches. In June 1903, President Theodore Roosevelt spoke here, while President William Howard Taft spoke here in 1911. The station was active into the late 1960s as a railroad office, but was sold to Cedar Lumber in 1969. It became the Depot Restaurant in 1972, but closed in 1986 and was remodeled as a bank.

The Rock Island depot isn't big, but it housed from the west a men's waiting room, an office for the station agent, a women's waiting room, and a baggage room to the east. Across the street to the south was a warehouse for the International Harvester Company of America, served by the railroad. To the east on the northeast corner of State & Sixth was the CRIP Freight House.

In 1953, the railroad had an 87-car yard at Cedar Falls, along with a siding that could hold 28 cars. Cedar Falls also served as a train order station.

While the tracks between Waterloo and Cedar Falls are gone, the former Rock Island stations still stand at each community. The one at Cedar Falls is along Fifth Street where the mainline once ran down the center of the street.

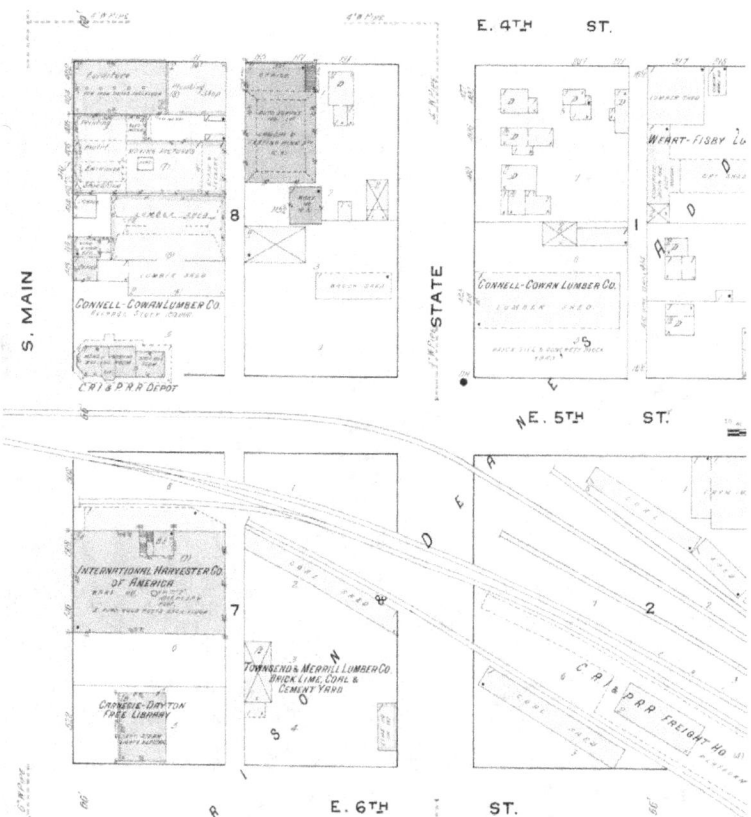

This Sanborn map from 1916 shows the Rock Island passenger station at Cedar Falls, located at the intersection of Fifth and Main streets. Behind the depot was the Connell-Cowan Lumber Company, while across the tracks was a warehouse for the International Harvester Company. *Sanborn Fire Insurance Map from Cedar Falls, Black Hawk County, Iowa.* Sanborn Map Company, January 1916. Map. Retrieved from the Library of Congress, https://www.loc.gov/item/sanborn02596_006/.

These weren't the only station and freight houses in downtown Cedar Falls. At the east end of Fourth Street was the Chicago Great Western passenger and freight depot. A separate freight house was located to the south.

119

For the four blocks west of here, the tracks run down the middle of Fifth Street. Much of this route is through a residential area. Leaving Fifth Street at Franklin Street, the railroad curves behind a number of homes before reaching the Canadian National mainline at Cedar Falls Junction.

On June 24, 2012, an excursion train on the Iowa Northern loaded its passengers on the Fifth Street trackage in Iowa City. At one end was IANR #678 in its Rock Island-inspired paint.

At the other end of the train was IANR #461, parked in the middle of Fifth Street.

157.5 CEDAR FALLS JUNCTION – This is the connection between the CN and IANR's former Rock Island Route. At one time there was a diamond here, but today the connection and crossing use turnouts. To the south is the Cedar Falls Spur, while to the north is the mainline of the Manly Subdivision. Heading north, the tracks are on the bank of the Cedar River for the next mile.

160.5 BEAVER CREEK BRIDGE – Beaver Creek starts about 25 miles to the west and flows into the Cedar River just to the east of the tracks. This is a 175-foot through truss bridge with timber trestles on each end. The truss was built by the American Bridge Company of New York in 1927. Look for the mark indicating the 2008 high water level at about the center of the bridge on the west side. Sitting in a railroad passenger car, water would be up close to your knees.

To the north of the bridge, a lake to the west has the name Railroad Lake. In reality, much of this large wooded area is a series of wetlands, lakes, and streams. It has historically been a problem area for the railroad due to high and standing water.

161.3 NORRIS – Norris was listed in early Rock Island timetables, but was not assigned a station code in the *1910 List of Officers and Station Agents*. Look for the road crossing that heads into the Falls Access hunting area. There is sign of a grade to the east side of the tracks. The railroad had a 79-car-long siding here in 1953. A. J. Norris once owned land in the area.

North of Norris at Milepost 162.5 is a short spur track known as MOW (Maintenance of Way) Spur Track. The road crossing is known as Rotary Crossing for the Rotary Reserve meeting facility to the east. The Rotary Reserve is managed by the Black Hawk County Conservation Board and the Waterloo Rotary Club. Funding for the lodge was provided by members of the Waterloo Rotary Club and was constructed by personnel of the Black Hawk County Conservation Board.

164.7 WINSLOW – Winslow was listed in early Rock Island timetables, but was not assigned a station code in the *1910 List of Officers and Station Agents*. During the 1950s, this was known as Winslow Spur and was shown to have a capacity of 15 cars.

Look for the Winslow Road grade crossing. Maps from 1910 show that there were several houses here with a school not far west of the tracks. This was an important route at the time because Winslow Road had one of the few bridges in the area that crossed the Cedar River.

165.1 WEST FORK CEDAR RIVER BRIDGE – The West Fork is formed when several streams flow together just south of Mason City. The river then flows to the southeast for about 40 miles before flowing into the Cedar River several miles to the southeast of here.

The original through truss span bridge was built in 1894, replacing a bridge built during the 1870s. Many years ago, a train derailed while passing through the span and several plates were welded on to strengthen damaged components. During and after the 2008 floods, trains used this route that normally didn't need to. One of the results of this was the discovery that modern autoracks will not fit through the bridge, discovered when one lost its roof while passing through the truss span.

Because of the age of the bridge, the railroad limited the weight of loads that could move over the bridge. Therefore, the bridge was replaced starting in October 2010, with the new bridge in place and opening on March 3, 2011. The truss span was replaced with two 95-foot through plate girder spans, providing wider clearances and no upper height limit. The north end of the bridge still includes 336 feet of ballast deck timber spans for a total bridge length of 526 feet. IANR documents show the bridge to be named Thomsen's Bridge.

Heading north, trains climb a grade of more than 1% for the next mile.

165.6 COUNTY LINE – Look for the Marquis Road crossing, shown as Bluebird Avenue on some maps, as the county line is just south of there. **Black Hawk County**, located to the south, was created in 1843 and named for the Sac war leader who lost the war that bears his name (and who never set foot in the area named for him). However, with no permanent population, the county was first administered by Delaware County (1843-1845), then Benton County (1845-1851), and then Buchanan County (1851-1853). In 1853, Black Hawk County was allowed to organize its own government and elect officers, making Waterloo its county seat.

Meanwhile, in 1845, at a ford in the river that had long been used by Indian tribes, settlers George and Mary Hanna created the community of Prairie Rapids that attracted other settlers. At about the same time, a mill was built nearby at what was called Sturgis Falls. Thus Sturgis Falls and Prairie Rapids, later to be renamed Cedar Falls and Waterloo, became in 1845 the first settlements in Black Hawk County, and between them at the end of the year they boasted the county's entire white population of thirteen pioneers.

Surrounded by some of the richest farmland to be found anywhere on the globe, the cities of Black Hawk County became important centers for the agricultural community. Despite a brief period of high water, which allowed the steamboat *Black Hawk* to make twenty-four round trips between Cedar Rapids and Waterloo in 1859, the Cedar River was not destined to provide a transportation advantage. Thus, it was the arrival of railroads that opened up the nation's markets to the farms of Black Hawk County.

Today, Black Hawk County is Iowa's fifth-most populous county, with 131,144 residents reported in the 2020 census.

North of here is **Bremer County**. The first white man came to Bremer County in 1845 and settled about two miles southwest of Denver, Iowa. At that time this area was a reservation belonging to the Winnebago Tribe. Later the reservation was purchased by the government and the Native Americans were moved to the Crow River area of Minnesota, about 150 miles north of St. Paul.

In 1850, Bremer County was originally organized and named for Swedish writer Frederika Bremer by Governor Hempstead, who was an admirer of the Swedish authoress. Bremer County is thought to be the only Iowa county named after a person eminent in literature.

Today's county seat, Waverly, was first settled in 1850, and soon became important due to its waterpower that was used by flour and saw mills. On January 24, 1853, Waverly was chosen as the county seat. Later that year in August, Bremer County was permanently organized with the election of county officers. Unlike many counties in the state, the county seat has remained unchanged. The county is mostly rural and had a population of 24,988 in the 2020 census.

167.9 WAVERLY JUNCTION – The Rock Island had a branch that headed northeast from here to serve Waverly, Iowa, opened in 1886. The railroad was built by the Waverly Short Line Railroad Company, incorporated on June 6, 1885. The incorporation statement was almost as long as the six-mile-long railroad, but it also included a "telegraph or telephone line or both." The Burlington, Cedar Rapids & Northern leased the company by 1893, and purchased it on May 22, 1902. In 1953, the railroad had a track here with the capacity of 22 cars. The line was abandoned in December 1959. The old grade can barely be made out curving to the northeast near the grade crossing with 265th Street.

169.5 COUNTY LINE – Heading towards Manly, the railroad has turned to the northwest, crossing from **Bremer County** to **Butler County**. The county line is south of the 250th Street grade crossing. **Butler County** was named in honor of General William Orlando Butler, a Kentucky statesman, officer in the Mexican War, and unsuccessful Democratic candidate for Vice President in 1848. Before the county was officially organized, it was attached to other counties. But by 1853, enough settlers had located in Butler County to warrant setting up the county's own government, and an election was held in August. Interestingly enough, although a full staff of county officials was elected, the offices were not considered sufficiently lucrative to warrant a trip to Independence to be sworn in, so the elected officers failed to qualify. Therefore, another election was held in August 1854, and this time the elected officials took the oath of office and the county took over the governing of its own territory.

The county seat of Butler County has moved around a bit based upon which community had the political power at the time. The first county seat was Clarksville, and then in 1859 it was moved to Butler Center until a court ordered a new election, which again selected Butler Center in 1860. According to A. T. Andreas in his *1875 Illustrated Historical Atlas of the State of Iowa*, Butler Center was, except for it being the county seat, "a place of no commercial or other importance." Andreas continued, "The village contains, besides the court house, so called, two general stores, and wagon and blacksmith shops. The best public structure in the place is a two-story frame school house, 20x40, capable of seating 160 pupils..."

Because of the sad conditions that existed at Butler Center, further efforts were made to move the county seat. Clarksville again sought to obtain the county seat, as did Bristow and Shell Rock, all without success. With the coming of the Dubuque & Dakota Railroad (CGW) to Butler County in 1879, the town of Allison (located a few miles west of Clarksville), named for United States Senator William B. Allison, was platted and was successful, after several elections, in having the courthouse built there in 1881 at a cost of $10,680.

The population of Butler County is less than 15,000, and it reportedly is the only county in Iowa that does not have a four-lane road, a stop light, a hospital, or a movie theater. Reports also indicate that there are no national fast-food chains in the county.

172.2 SHELL ROCK – Shell Rock is located to the north, and was named for the Shell Rock River which flows through the center of town. The town was founded in March 1855 by George and Elizabeth Adair, and a post office opened that year. The community was incorporated on June 1, 1875. The initial focus was on the river, and a mill dam that was used by several mills and an electric plant still can be seen in the river upstream of the Cherry Street bridge. Standing next to the Cherry Street bridge is "The Old Mill," a five-story mill built by the Adair family in 1867. The mill operated until 1978 and has since been turned into a private home.

Shell Rock was the childhood home for a few years of Lou Henry Hoover, leader of the Girl Scouts during the 1920s and 1930s, a well-known geologist, and a noted philanthropist. She was also the first lady of the United States from 1929 to 1933 as the wife of President Herbert Hoover.

This marker in downtown Shell Rock, Iowa, notes the one-time presence of Lou Henry Hoover, America's First Lady during the early 1930s.

Shell Rock is also famous for its Shell Rock Music Association. The group was formed in 1964 when Iowa Governor Hughes suggested that each Iowa community create a program to welcome new teachers. The program created a series of musical performances which have continued to today, consisting of various types of shows held in the Boyd Building.

The Railroad at Shell Rock

The railroad erected a depot at Shell Rock as soon as the railroad was built. It was located north of Cherry Street on the east side of the mainline. There was a siding to the west and a house track that looped around the east side of the station. On this track was the railroad's stockyards, several small sheds and warehouses, Bement Lumber and an elevator further north where the Farmer's Coop now stands. It was noted that this early elevator was built in 1885 and had a capacity of 16,000 bushels.

In 1953, the Shell Rock station had a communications station that was open 8:30am-5:30pm. It also served as a train order station. The siding could hold 68 freight cars, and there were other tracks with a capacity of 62 freight cars.

The Shell Rock depot was still staffed by an agent in 1965. By 1974, the agent had been replaced by a simple company telephone. There was a 3411-foot-long siding and 2583 feet of other tracks. The Rock Island used the code "SH" for the station, which the Iowa Northern still uses. Shell Rock has an elevator track to the east and the 3168-foot West Shell Rock Track. They serve the Farmers Cooperative of Readlyn – Shell Rock. The cooperative has their fertilizer facility to the west and their elevator to the east.

The long West Shell Rock Track starts north of town near Lake Road, and its south switch is just south of Cherry Street, the way it has been for years. The population of Shell Rock is about 1300, and the size of the town is about what it was in 1917.

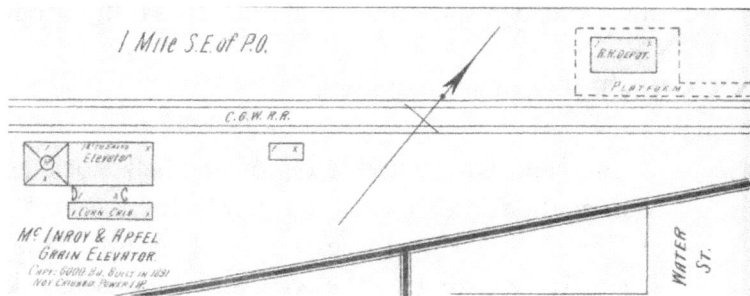

This Sanborn map from 1902 shows the Shell Rock depot, once located north of Cherry Street. *Sanborn Fire Insurance Map from Shell Rock, Butler County, Iowa.* Sanborn Map Company, March 1902. Map. Retrieved from the Library of Congress, https://www.loc.gov/item/sanborn02823_002/.

Shell Rock is still the home of an active grain elevator, the Farmers Cooperative of Readlyn – Shell Rock.

175.0 BUTLER – Northwest of Shell Rock is a new complex developed by the Iowa Northern Railway. Where once corn and soybeans were grown, now jobs and industry are growing. This new complex stretches from Old Iowa Highway 3 (220th Street at Milepost 174.3) to north of the highway overpass of Iowa Highway 3 at Milepost 175.5. The terminal is known as Butler ("BU") by the Iowa Northern Railway, but it includes the Butler Logistics Park and the Butler Intermodal Terminal. However, many of the companies that have located here still call the area Shell Rock, Iowa.

While the post office address of Butler Logistics Park is Shell Rock, the railroad calls the location Butler, as this station sign demonstrates.

The first rail customer at Butler came about when groundbreaking commenced on a new ethanol plant here in 2007. Known as the Butler plant and operated initially by Hawkeye Renewables, it was designed for a 110-million-gallon annual output and commenced shipping by the end of 2008. It was later sold to Flint Hills Resources. To handle this new plant, a new yard was built to the west and named Butler Yard (for the county in which it is located). The new yard included three tracks with a capacity of more than 150 cars. Additionally, an East Storage Track (7620 feet long) and a West Storage Track (5936 feet long) were built. Plans were also considered to build a 13-track yard with a capacity of just over 1000 cars, as well as a new locomotive shop and operating offices.

The 2008 flooding forced the Iowa Northern to alter some of their plans for this location. Badly needing a base to operate out of, they located a temporary office building at the south switch, off to the west side of the tracks. Crews still use this facility. The railroad also needed storage tracks since parts of the railroad were out of service. The siding to the west was quickly built, using secondhand rail and new steel ties. The complex has been expanded as the Butler Logistics Park.

During July 2019, IANR #461 was photographed switching the yard at Butler with the silos of the large ethanol plant in the background.

The ethanol plant was acquired by POET on June 1, 2021, becoming POET Bioprocessing – Shell

Rock. The facility produces 131 million gallons of bioethanol annually as well as livestock feed solutions. POET was founded in 1987 and has grown to include 34 bioprocessing facilities, all based out of the company's headquarters in Sioux Falls, South Dakota.

Other companies have located here, and the railroad promotes the Butler Logistics Park as a 92-acre site at the center of its railroad just north of Shell Rock. Facilities of American Colloid and Zinpro utilize 25 acres of the industrial park. The American Colloid Company is a part of Minerals Technologies Inc., and manufactures green sand bond solutions for ferrous castings, bentonite products, chemical binder systems, and similar products. American Colloid Company is especially known as one of the world's leading producers of bentonite clay, a product that can be used as a thickener, sealant, binder, lubricant or absorbtion agent. Minerals Technologies traces its history back to the 1840s while American Colloid has been serving the metalcasting industry since 1927.

Also west of the rail yard at Butler is Zinpro Corporation. This firm was founded in 1965, incorporated in 1971, and built its first manufacturing plant in 1993 at Garner, Iowa. This plant opened in 2013. The family-owned company manufactures organic trace minerals and produces nutritional health solutions for pets, livestock, and even people. These products are sold in more than 70 countries.

In June 2019, it was announced that TrinityRail would be locating a manufacturing and maintenance plant at the Butler Logistics Park, adding 230 acres to the complex. Grading of the site was underway by July, and the plant began operations by the end of 2020. When completed, the $60 million plant was the largest and most equipped maintenance facility in the Trinity Industries network. The facility includes 370,000 square feet of manufacturing floor space and seven miles of rail track. Work conducted includes car repairs and maintenance, including cleaning, inspections, testing, painting, air brake repairs, and full rebuilds.

In 2019, construction is underway on the large TrinityRail facility being built at the Butler Logistics Park.

South of TrinityRail is Shell Rock Soy Processing, a new soybean crush plant that will crush about 38.5 million bushels of soybeans annually, or 110,000 bushels daily. From this, it will produce roughly 847,000 tons per year of soybean meal, along with soy hulls for livestock feed, and soybean oil that may be used for a variety of applications, including livestock feed, fuel and the human food industry. A new long spur track was built to access this plant.

In late 2019, the Iowa Northern joined with Union Pacific, Watco Logistics (terminal operating), and Valor Victoria (freight forwarder) in announcing the creation of an Iowa-West Coast international intermodal service from Butler. In 2020, the group shipped the first 30 containers to Manly, where Union Pacific handled the movement on to the west coast. The facility is designed to fill containers that typically move west empty, and to avoid the congestion around Chicago terminals.

177.7 SHELL ROCK RIVER BRIDGE – This is a two-span Warren through truss bridge, built in 1921. There are also five deck plate girder spans, each 40 feet long, on the south end of the bridge. They were built in 1902. The Shell Rock River is a tributary of the Cedar River flowing south from Albert Lea Lake in Freeborn County, Minnesota. The IANR will follow the Shell Rock River northward for about 45 miles to near Plymouth. The United States Board on Geographic Names settled on "Shell Rock River" as the stream's name in 1931. It has also been known by the spelling "Shellrock River."

This two-span Warren through truss bridge is used to cross the Shell Rock River just a few miles south of Clarksville, Iowa.

178.2 MILL RIVER BRIDGE – Look for the 30-foot deck plate girder span. Mill River isn't recognized on many maps, but it is a series of ponds and streams on the south side of Clarksville that drains the area to the northeast of town. The adjacent road to the north is Mill Street, so it appears that there was a mill here at one time.

178.9 CNW CROSSING – This was a Chicago Great Western (CGW) line and a concrete block depot still remains on the route. The original CGW passenger and freight depot was on the north side of the track between Main and Mather. To the east and on the south side of the CGW tracks was the Muller and Brockmann elevator and lumber yard. The elevator was built in 1884 and had a 20,000-bushel capacity. There were stockyards further east on the south side, located east of Church Street.

In 1872, the Iowa Pacific Railroad (IP) graded a line through here, but didn't lay much track. This makes it the oldest CGW property. In the late 1870s, much of the IP's property was acquired by the Dubuque & Dakota (D&D), which laid tracks through here in 1879-1880. The Minnesota & Northwestern purchased the D&D in 1887, all of which later became part of the Chicago Great Western. The CGW was acquired by the Chicago & North Western in 1968, and this route was abandoned in 1989. The route east of here to Shell Rock is today the Butler County Nature Trail.

Today, the 1.7 miles of track to the east is known as the Bristow Spur. It serves the Bristow Spur Elevators, also shown as the Butler County Ag Facility on some maps. A part of the agricultural history of Clarksville in this area is the Schmadeke Feed Mill elevator. It was built in the early 1930s and started operations in 1934, although this wasn't the start of the Schmadeke businesses at Clarksville. The July 29, 1859, issue of *American Lumberman* reported that the firm Heery & Schmadeke had been succeeded by Schmadeke & Watland. Today, the feed mill is still used to grind and mix feed, and is now owned by the third generation of the Schmadeke family. The company buys and sells corn and soybeans, working with ethanol producers to provide low-cost fuel for Iowans and feed for livestock producers. In early 2020, Schmadeke's Feed Mill was one of the first firms to load containers that were shipped from the Butler Intermodal Terminal to the Port of Los Angeles and international markets.

There was once a diamond here with an interchange track in the southeast quadrant. While the diamond no longer exists, a connecting track comes in from the Iowa Northern from the north, where the Rock Island depot once stood. The interchange track from the south, with a switch at IANR Milepost 178.6, has now been cut and is used as a maintenance of way track.

179.2 CLARKSVILLE – Clarksville was named for its founders, Thomas Clark and Jeremiah Clark. They were members of the Clark-Poisal wagon train which traveled from Indiana to Iowa in 28 days, arriving here on July 6, 1852. The town was surveyed and founded in 1853, and the Clarksville post office opened in 1861. It was incorporated on May 11, 1874, located on the land of Thomas and Jeremiah Clark, Daniel Mather, and D. C. Hilton.

The first Butler County court was held at Clarksville in October 1854 in a little log hut in which its owner, Mr. Clark, sold groceries. Although there were earlier attempts to erect a courthouse, the first to be built was begun in 1856 and completed in 1858 at Clarksville. Located in a square near the center of town, this 40' x 60' two-story brick courthouse cost $20,000. However, it was sold to the local school district only four years later for a mere $2800 when the location of the county seat was changed. The building then served as a schoolhouse from 1863 to 1903, when it was torn down.

The Burlington, Cedar Rapids & Northern depot was located north of Jefferson Street and east of the tracks. It featured a long brick platform to the north of the depot. To the north of the depot was an elevator that went through several owners. It was built in 1886 and had a capacity of 20,000 bushels. By 1915, it was shown as "Elevator CRI&P Owners, Voss & Christensen Lessees." Across the tracks to the west was the Clarksville Co-Operative Creamery.

During the 1950s, Clarksville was the home of a siding with a capacity of 106 cars. The various industry tracks could hold 33 freight cars. The depot housed a train order station. Clarksville has always been assigned the station code "CU". To the west is the Clarksville Storage Track. The station at Clarksville had no shippers in 1994; it now has three separate companies loading: Peavey, Shear, and United Suppliers, which collectively amount to 15 percent of IANR-originated grain. In addition, there has been talk about a new pulp and paper mill designed to convert corn stover (corn stalks).

Clarksville is smaller today than in 1917, and almost the entire town is to the east of the tracks. Its population was 1,264 during the 2020 census. However, it still features its own school system and several stores and gas stations.

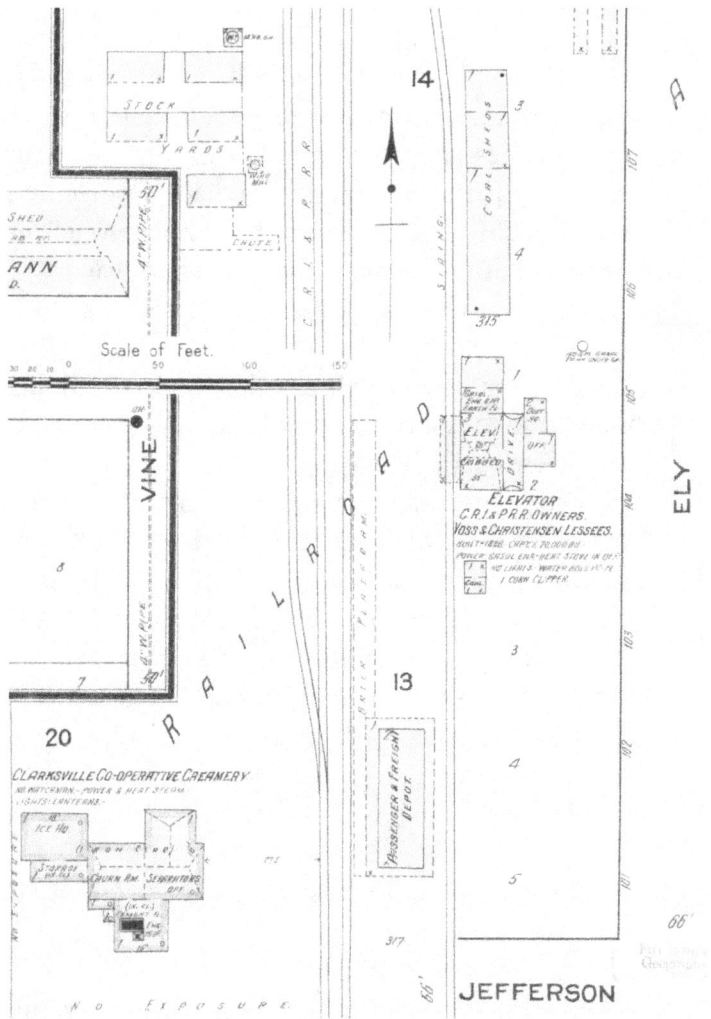

The Rock Island depot at Clarksville was located on the east side of the tracks, north of Jefferson Street. This Sanborn map from 1915 also showed the Clarksville Cooperative Creamery, located west of the station for several decades. *Sanborn Fire Insurance Map from Clarksville, Butler County, Iowa.* Sanborn Map Company, November 1915. Map. Retrieved from the Library of Congress, https://www.loc.gov/item/sanborn02606_004/.

183.8 FLOOD CREEK BRIDGE – Flood Creek flows in from the north and is crossed using a deck plate girder span. On June 2, 1916, at 3:10 am, a northbound Rock Island passenger train (No. 19) fell through the Flood Creek bridge during high water conditions. Photos and newspaper reports indicate that several steel coaches and chair cars fell into the river and that 17 of their occupants drowned, reportedly all from the single coach car that completely fell into the waters. Rescuers came from as far away as Waterloo, and a reported 50,000 spectators visited the site over the next several days.

Earlier in the evening, other trains had been halted due to the rains and flooding. Repairs of the track were made between Packard and Greene, not far north of here. After an inspection of the railroad, No. 19 headed north with passengers from the other delayed trains, following a work and inspection train, which crossed Flood Creek at about 2:35am.

Following the derailment, the bridge was replaced by a wooden trestle. Today, the bridge consists of three deck plate girder spans built in 1929 by the American Bridge Company of New York. It is 170 feet long.

185.1 PACKARD – The Rock Island didn't have a station code for Packard in 1910, and in 1953 there were only several side tracks with a total capacity of 26 freight cars. However, today the Iowa Northern uses "PK". The Packard Elevator Track is to the west. Packard Elevator is part of the Innovative Ag Services Company (IAS). The company dates back to 1969 when the Swiss Valley Ag Service was created. Through the construction of new facilities and mergers with other agricultural businesses, the company grew and Innovative Ag Services was created in July 2005. The Packard elevator was bought in August 2007. Mergers and acquisitions continued, and now IAS has facilities scattered across northern Iowa. The Packard location offers bagged feed, a full-service tire shop, 2,034,000 bushels of grain storage and drying capabilities, and a 14-car grain rail load-out on the Iowa Northern. Innovative Ag Services sold the Packard elevator in 2021.

Joseph Packard bought a farm in the area in 1865 and arrived to work the property in 1867. Postal records show that a post office opened at Packard in 1876, a few years after the railroad was built through the community. The town was a typical small farming community with a blacksmith, general store, church, and a few other businesses. A grain elevator opened at Packard in 1901. A map from 1917 shows that Packard was a small town two blocks wide east to west, and three blocks south from the railroad, all east of the Packard Avenue grade crossing. In that same year, the Packard post office closed.

190.0 GREENE – The first town in the area was named Elm Springs, platted in 1855 by John Hardman and John Miller, and later owned by T. T. Rawson. Located south of the Shell Rock River, there was an Elm Springs post office there from 1857 to 1871 when it was moved to the new town on the railroad route.

John W. Miller bought the site where Greene now stands in 1854, opened a small inn and served as the postmaster of Elm Springs until his death in 1856. The land was sold to the Eikenberry family, who sold it to the Burlington, Cedar Rapids & Minnesota Railway Company (BCR&M) for a townsite. It was soon named Greene for Judge George Greene, president of the BCR&M, who paid for the construction of a library. Greene played many roles in Iowa, including lawyer, justice of the Iowa Supreme Court, railroad entrepreneur, businessman, philanthropist, and one of the founders of Cedar Rapids, Iowa. Greene was also president of the Burlington, Cedar Rapids & Minnesota Railroad, and later the Burlington, Cedar Rapids & Northern Railroad.

In September 1871, the town was platted. Within a month, the town had a population of more than fifty with several stores, a grain elevator, warehouse, and lumberyard. The Elm Springs post office moved to the new town in 1871, using the name Green. *The Butler County Press* began publishing newspapers in Greene in 1873, and almost immediately published that "In 1873 Greene has a population of 500, one church, a good schoolhouse, one drug store, one shoe store, one planing mill, one wagon factory, four dry goods and grocery stores, two harness shops, two hotels, two millinery stores, two banks, two agricultural warehouses, two blacksmith shops, three grain warehouses, two lumberyards, two saloons and one restaurant, a town library." In 1876, the post office changed the spelling of its name from Green to Greene. With the growth of the community, Greene was incorporated on July 15, 1879.

The Shell Rock River bisects the town, and in 1875, the Wanatah Mill and its dam opened on the river. Because the dam washed out several times, it went through several owners until 1908 when the Greene Electric Light & Power Company acquired it. The dam still stands just south of the Traer Street bridge.

By 1900, the population of Greene had reached 1192. A 1917 map of Greene showed that the "Original Town" extended five blocks along the railroad, and two blocks west to the Shell Rock River and three blocks east. The town had apparently grown quickly as Traer's Addition and Traer's 2nd Addition were across the Shell Rock River while Thorp's Addition and McClure's 1st Addition were to the north of the original plat. To the south and on both sides of the tracks was the Railroad Addition. The population grew slowly until it reached 1427 in the 1960 census.

The population of Greene was 1130 in 2010, and then 990 in 2020. Greene was once the home of Thomas Braden, author of the book *Eight Is Enough*, the inspiration for the television show of the same name. The Greene Historical Museum is located across from Perrin Park in an early 1900s boarding house, just north of downtown. Probably more important for most rail enthusiasts is the preserved Rock Island depot. Records show that the station was built in 1872 by the BCR&N, and the wooden two-story structure is similar to several others on the line. The Iowa Northern donated the station in 1988 and it was moved to 311 North Second Street and restored. It houses a number of railroad displays and memorabilia. CNW caboose #11086 is on display nearby. The former Packard, Iowa, depot was moved to the south end of town in Greene many years ago and turned into an office.

Dow Street is the center of Greene today. To the northwest is the elevator complex of Landus, which dates its history back to 1888 with the development of the Farmers Elevator and Livestock Company in Jordan, Iowa. Since then, dozens of elevators, grain companies, feed millers, mill suppliers, agronomy facilities, a hardware store and an energy company have merged, eventually forming Landus in 2016. Today, Landus is a farmer-owned cooperative that provides grain storage, dry and liquid fertilizers, bulk crop protection, and rail loading. Over the past few years, the old grain elevators to the east have been removed.

"GN" was and is the station code for the station. Greene was a train order station in 1953, and there was a 73-car siding and industry tracks with a capacity of 72 cars. Today, there is both an East and a West Elevator Track at Greene. Greene is important enough to have yard limits (Milepost 189.0-191.0). Greene was the early headquarters of the Iowa Northern. Looking to the west, a two-story white building at 113 North Second Street can be seen with IANR lettering. There is also the newer office building on the southwest corner of the grade crossing with Dow Street, once the home of the railroad's dispatcher.

Greene, Iowa, has a number of railroad structures, including the former Rock Island two-story depot. Parked nearby is former Chicago & North Western caboose #11086.

At 113 North Second Street in Greene, Iowa, is this building with IANR lettering, once the office for the railroad.

The tracks through Greene are lined by a series of grain elevators, often with covered hoppers nearby for loading.

With the grain movements at Greene, it is not uncommon to find Iowa Northern power in town. In May 2012, these locomotives were there to build a train for movement to an online ethanol plant.

190.8 COUNTY LINE – The county line is located at the grade crossing with Floyd Line Street, with **Butler County** to the south and **Floyd County** to the north.

Floyd County was established in January 1851 and officially organized as of August 1854. Where the name Floyd came from is unknown, but there are at least three explanations. The first, and probably the most widely-held belief is that the county was named for Sergeant Charles Floyd, a member of the famed Lewis and Clark Expedition, who died in 1804 during the trip and was buried just south of present-day Sioux City. His death and burial were the first ever recorded in Iowa.

A second explanation is that Floyd County was named in honor of William Floyd of Long Island, New York, one of the signers of the Declaration of Independence. A third explanation is that the county was named after former Virginia governor and Secretary of War, John Buchanan Floyd. This latter explanation caused some to try to rename the county after John Buchanan Floyd joined the Confederate Army as a general during the Civil War. That effort was aborted, though, after Senator John F. Duncombe of Fort Dodge assured people that the county was indeed named after Charles Floyd.

In 2020, the county's population was 15,627. Its county seat is Charles City.

194.4 GRAVEL PIT NO. 1 – This location was listed as a station in the 1910s but was gone by the 1960s. The small gravel pit was located between the grade crossings with Jersey Avenue (Milepost 194.3) and 280th Street (Milepost 194.5).

195.5 MARBLE ROCK – Marble Rock was founded in October 1856, the post office opened in 1859, and the town was incorporated on February 8, 1881. It was named for a local white limestone formation that looked like marble. Assigned station code "RA", today there is a Fertilizer Track and a Storage Track to the east and an Elevator Track to the west. Viafield operates the large grain elevator to the west. It has a capacity of 1,950,000 bushels, and the company also sells liquid chemicals, liquid and dry fertilizers, and anhydrous. Viafield is a member-owned ag cooperative in northern Iowa and southern Minnesota, dating back to the 1891 creation of the Farmers Cooperative Exchange of Rockford. Through the mergers of dozens of elevators and cooperatives, three organizations were formed: Progressive Ag, Farmers Co-op, and Northeast Iowa Co-op. In 2010, they merged to create Viafield. On September 12, 2023, the farmer members of Northern Country Cooperative and Viafield voted to merge the two agriculture retail companies. The new cooperative began conducting unified business effective February 1, 2024.

During July 2006, IANR #3810 heads south between the co-op buildings at Marble Rock, Iowa.

Marble Rock is in the middle of a long tangent track from near Milepost 192 to near Milepost 201. In 1911, Marble Rock became a railroad junction when the Charles City Western Railway (CCW) reached here from Charles City. The railroad was created by local promoters in Charles City, who felt that the more railroads the better, wanting more competition for Illinois Central and the Milwaukee Road railroads. The line originally operated steam freight service and passenger service using a McKeen gas-powered motorcar. With the boom in electric interurbans, the CCW was electrified in 1915. By 1952, passenger service ended and the railroad survived due to freight. On December 31, 1963, the CCW was acquired by the Iowa Terminal Railroad and was operated as the Charles City Division. The Charles City Division was dieselized after a tornado destroyed much of the overhead lines on May 15, 1968. Several years later the remaining trackage was abandoned. The old grade can be seen curving to the northeast behind the fertilizer building at the north end of town.

The Moore & Hoover Marble Rock Elevator opened in 1872. The Marble Rock Creamery opened in 1882 and shipped almost 10,000 pounds of butter each month to New York. It was located on the east side of the tracks at the north end of town. The town also featured many of the typical businesses such as general stores, drug stores, saloons, a bank, and lumber yards. The west side of the railroad was full of lumber yards and grain elevators by the late 1800s. In 1895, the Gates & Bucklen Lumber Company was located south of Bradford Street, also designated 270th Street. The Marble Rock Elevator Company was located north of Bradford Street. The railroad depot was further north, with a poultry house west of the depot. Heading on west, there was a grain house with a 60,000-bushel grain elevator, and a stockyard.

In 1899, a 60,000-bushel grain elevator was built just north of the depot and the stockyard was moved to the east, across from the depot. By 1902, the Marble Rock Elevator Company was known as the Bucklen Grain Company. Both elevators were the Bucklen Taber Company by 1910. The lumber yard was by then Fred Gates Lumber.

While Marble Rock was never a large community, it was still the site of one of the longest sidings on the railroad during the 1950s. The siding was 83 cars long, plus there were other tracks with a capacity of 46 cars. There was also a train order station in the depot. These facilities probably were due to the junction with the Charles City Western Railway.

Today, Marble Rock is no larger than it was more than 100 years ago. The population of Marble Rock was 307 in the 2010 census, and 271 at the time of the 2020 census. To the west several blocks is the

Marble Rock Dam on the Shell Rock River. The dam was built in 1914 and is one of the landmarks left by these earlier industries.

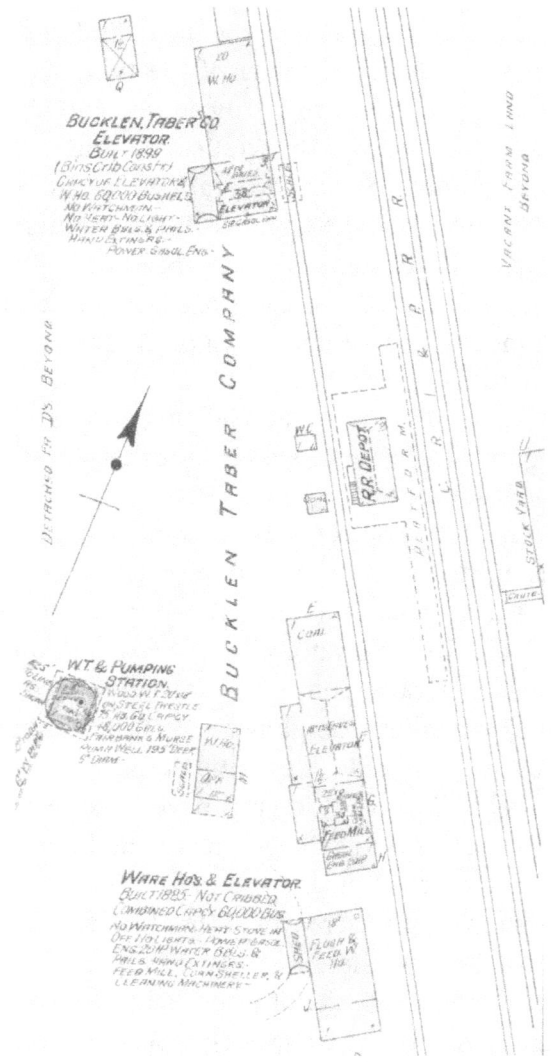

In 1910, Marble Falls featured a typical railroad depot and the large Bucklen Taber grain and elevator operation. *Sanborn Fire Insurance Map from Marble Rock, Floyd County, Iowa.* Sanborn Map Company, December 1910. Map. Retrieved from the Library of Congress, https://www.loc.gov/item/sanborn02738_003/.

202.6 SHELL ROCK RIVER BRIDGE – Also known by some as IANR Shell Rock River Bridge #2, this is another deck plate girder bridge, very common on this line. The bridge spans were built in 1898, and the 280-foot-long bridge consists of four deck plate girder spans. A unique feature is that the north and south spans feature fishbelly ends so they fit on the bridge's headwalls.

The Shell Rock River bridge is at the bottom of 1% grades in each direction. Several thousand feet to the south of the bridge, the Winnebago River flows into the Shell Rock River.

203.6 ROCKFORD – Coming into the City of Rockford from the south, the railroad winds its way through a half-dozen blocks of homes before reaching a tall grain elevator complex. Rockford, Iowa, was founded in 1856 by George Wyatt and three investors from Rockford, Illinois, which quickly grew by the addition of several additional investors. The Rockford post office also opened in 1855. The parties contracted to have a dam built on the Shell Rock River later that year and had a sawmill in operation by fall. This sawmill gave the community an advantage as most lumber had to be hauled in from a great distance away. Rockford was once the location of several dams, none of which still exist. In 1872, a dam was built for a grist mill. In 2010, the Iowa Department of Natural Resources determined the dam was in a state of failure, and in 2014, the dam was removed and the river returned to a free-flowing state.

The name Rockford was an obvious choice based upon where the founders were from. However, some sources also quote the rocky ford across the Shell Rock River. The first grain elevator in Rockford opened in 1875, and after a vote, Rockford was incorporated on March 19, 1878. The Rockford Creamery opened in 1882 and shipped butter to eastern markets. During the early days, Rockford grew quickly from 300 residents in 1860 to 700 in 1880, and then it peaked in the 1900 census at 1080 residents.

During the early 1890s, Rockford was a busy station for the railroad. The original station, which still stands, had a water tower at its north end. Across the tracks to the west and a short distance to the south was the 1800-bushel grain elevator of D. D. Cutler. This was the first elevator at Rockford, built in 1875 by R. F. Bacon. Dell D. Cutler bought half interest in the elevator in May 1876. Bacon sold his half interest to A. W. Dawson in February 1879. Dawson then sold his interest to Robert Lindon in June 1882. Cutler and Lindon shipped 225 carloads of corn, 135 carloads of oats, wheat and flax, and 94 carloads of livestock in 1882.

To the north of Cutler's elevator was a series of warehouses shown to be owned by Rockford Banking. Next was the Farmers Exchange grain elevator. On April 8, 1891, thirty-six farmers formed the Farmer's Exchange Company and built a new elevator. The Rockford cooperative was reportedly the first co-op established in Iowa. Across all of the tracks to the east were stockyards. Here, there were four tracks, two on each side of the depot. Also in the center of the four tracks was a fifth track, shown as an incline track, elevated 14 feet for locomotive coaling.

Within a few years, the Cutler elevator was the Rockford Elevator Company, and an ice house had been built to the east of the depot. Things continued to change as the Ober & Kingsbury Grain Company was operating the southernmost elevator, and improvements had been made on the railroad's coaling facility, adding improved coaling stations and an office. During the 1910s, a 3/4-mile spur track was built from the northwest side of town southward. It crossed the Lime River, now the Winnebago River, to reach the Rockford Brick & Tile Company. The original Cutler elevator was gone, as well as the locomotive coaling facility, within another decade or so.

The growth of Rockford ended about 1900, but the Farmer's Exchange Company continued to grow as it built new facilities. It was reorganized as the Farmers' Cooperative Exchange on November 29, 1950. In 1953, it built a large feed warehouse. The Exchange built a new 168-foot tall, 250,000-bushel, concrete elevator in 1955, and then doubled its capacity in 1959. It also added many other silos, fertilizer storage, and other facilities over the years.

The population of Rockford in 2010 was 860, and 758 in 2020. The town is scenic with its wooded residential areas and the Shell Rock River through its downtown. There are several stores and businesses in town, and the Rockford Public School has its classrooms at the east end of town.

For fossil collectors, Rockford is a common destination. Just west of town is the Floyd County Fossil and Prairie Park Center, the former clay pit for the Rockford Brick & Tile Company. Floyd County bought the clay pit in 1990 and created the county park to allow fossil collectors to explore the site. The pit has been described as a world-class fossil collecting locale and it is one of the few geological preserves in the United States where admission is free and collecting fossils for private use is allowed.

Rockford was once the home of Robert James Waller, former Dean of the School of Business at the University of Northern Iowa. Waller is probably best known for his book *The Bridges of Madison County.*

The Railroad at Rockford

The tracks of the Iowa Northern Railway are on the west side of Rockford, passing through grain elevators that can be seen for miles. Rockford is a favorite railroad photo location since the restored two-story wooden depot still stands, originally built in the 1870s. The railroad built through Rockford in 1872 and the station was built soon after. The station was typical for the era and featured living quarters upstairs for the station master. Next to the station is Illinois Central caboose #9528, later Illinois Central Gulf #199528. The caboose with wide vision cupola was built in 1968.

The station has been assigned the code of "RD" since at least 1910. The Rockford Elevator Track is to the west while the old house track is to the east. To the west at the restored railroad station is the Rockford Elevator, which dates back to the original 1875 elevator. On August 6, 1891, 36 farmers joined to form the Rockford Alliance and its Farmer's Exchange Company, making the Rockford Cooperative the first co-op established in Iowa. For years, the concrete elevator was painted Rockford Farmers Co-op Exchange, a name created in a 1950 reorganization. The cooperative is now part of Viafield and has the ability to store 1,400,000 bushels of grain.

In 1953, the Rock Island had a train order station at Rockford. There were side tracks with a capacity of 87 freight cars, plus a 67-car-long siding. The

Iowa Northern showed that there was 1151 feet of storage capacity during the early 2010s.

Rockford is known for its two-story Rock Island depot, still well maintained and located right next to the tracks.

In 2006, IANR #3810 passes the Rockford water tower as it heads south leading a freight train.

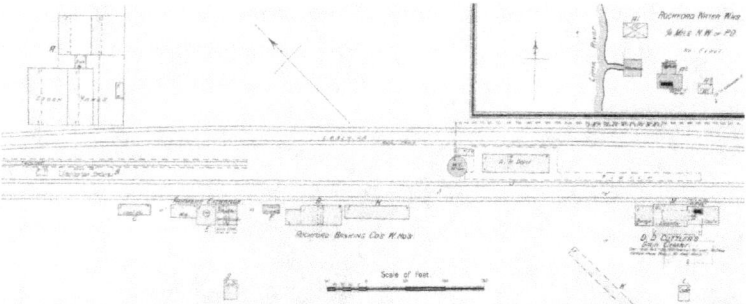

This Sanborn map from 1894 shows the Rockford railroad depot, and the grain elevators that surrounded it. *Sanborn Fire Insurance Map from Rockford, Floyd County, Iowa.* Sanborn Map Company, August 1894. Map. Retrieved from the Library of Congress https://www.loc.gov/item/sanborn02809_001/.

207.4 180TH STREET – After heading to the northwest since Shell Rock, the railroad has turned northward towards Nora Springs. This grade crossing is in the middle of miles of open farmland and the Shell Rock River is still several miles to the east.

208.7 AVENUE OF THE SAINTS – The railroad again passes under the Avenue of the Saints, a 563-mile-long highway between St. Louis, Missouri, and St. Paul, Minnesota. Here, it follows the route of U.S. Highway 18. Because of the confusion created by the Avenue of the Saints using a series of different numbered highways, in Iowa it is also known as Iowa Highway 27.

As the railroad has headed west, it has slowly been climbing. For example, where the railroad bridges the Shell Rock River at Rockford, the line's elevation was 1001 feet. Here it is about 1055 feet, and as the railroad approaches Nora Springs, it reaches 1087 feet.

IANR #3810 is heading south just before passing under U.S. Highway 18, known here as the Avenue of the Saints.

210.3 HAWKEYE AVENUE – The railroad crosses over Hawkeye Avenue, here a one-lane dirt road, using a beautiful stone arch, with smaller stone openings on either side of the road. The stone masonry arch is listed on the Iowa Historic Bridge Inventory and is shown to be 28 feet long. It was placed on the National Register of Historic Places in 1998. The Iowa Department of Transportation has the following description of the structure on its website.

> *This unique underpass was built by the Rock Island Line in 1889 to carry its tracks over South Hawkeye Street in Nora Springs, apparently during an upgrade of the area's rail lines. Supported by stone abutments, the stone arch grade separation continues to function today, in unaltered, well-preserved condition. This structure is the only stone arch bridge listed on the Iowa Historic Bridge*

Inventory in Floyd County, thus making it a rare and historically significant example of an early highway- and railroad-related resource.

210.7 CPRS CROSSING – This automatic interlocking is a diamond with the Iowa, Chicago & Eastern, now a part of Canadian Pacific. In Rock Island days, this was known as CMSTP&P Crossing. It is located southwest of Nora Springs, Iowa.

The McGregor & Sioux City Railway, incorporated January 23, 1868, built into Nora Springs from the east in 1869. Renamed the McGregor & Missouri River Railway, the railway built further west in 1870 using available land grants. It was soon absorbed by its parent company, the Milwaukee & St. Paul, which became the Chicago, Milwaukee & St. Paul Railway (CM&StP) in 1874. The CM&StP declared bankruptcy in 1925 and reorganized as the Chicago, Milwaukee, St. Paul & Pacific Railroad in 1928. Today, this line runs between Marquette and Sheldon, Iowa.

There is a connecting track in the northeast quadrant of the diamond. This can be an important connection as the Canadian Pacific operates via trackage rights over a nine-mile stretch of IANR between Nora Springs and Plymouth. This routing provides a shortcut for CP trains operating between Austin, Minnesota, and Marquette, Iowa, bypassing Mason City. This agreement began with the Soo Line in the late 1980s and has been handed down over time as the Austin-Marquette line changed operators: Canadian Pacific; I&M Rail Link; Iowa, Chicago & Eastern Railroad (IC&E); and finally back to Canadian Pacific. The Canadian Pacific typically operates two or more trains each way per day over this route. There was once a connecting track in the southwest quadrant and there has been some discussion about putting it back in.

The discussion to put the connecting track back in is due to the acquisition of the former CRIP line to Forest City, located west of Mason City. The IANR has obtained trackage rights over the CP, enabling the Iowa Northern to move freight between the connection of the Forest City Line and their mainline.

Nora Junction

The Burlington, Cedar Rapids & Minnesota Railway Company (BCR&M) reached here in 1872 and a station at the crossing opened almost immediately. A map from 1875 showed an active area at what was known as Nora Junction. The map showed a second connection between the two railroads in the southwest quadrant, with several blocks of a platted community where Larson's Salvage now stands. The map also showed a joint depot in the southwest corner of the diamond, and a hotel across the Rock Island tracks. The community of Nora Junction featured a grain warehouse.

Located on the southwest side of the diamond was an L-shaped wooden station. The station was staffed by a ticket and freight agent who worked for the BCR&M, and later for the Rock Island Railroad. South of the crossing were several buildings, a railroad bunkhouse, and stockyards. There were many early reports about livestock moving over the railroad from the Nora Junction stockyard.

In 1953, the railroad operated a train order station at Nora Springs. There was also a 66-car siding and others tracks with a capacity of 20 freight cars. Little of this remains today.

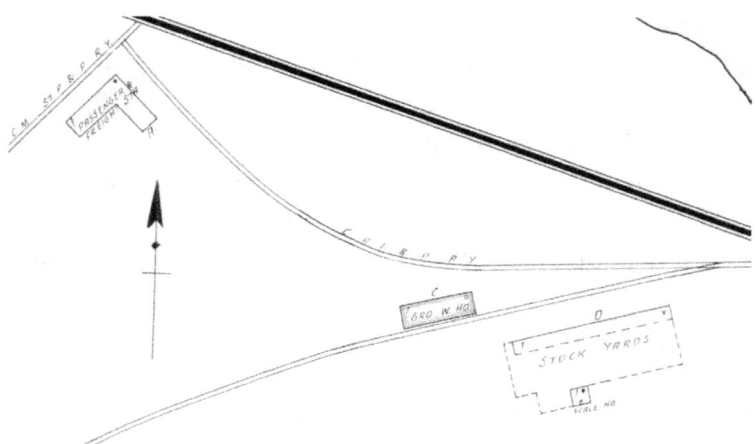

For years, a joint passenger and freight station stood at Nora Junction. The stockyards provided a large number of carloads of business for the Rock Island. *Sanborn Fire Insurance Map from Nora Springs, Floyd County, Iowa.* Sanborn Map Company, March 1942. Map. Retrieved from the Library of Congress, https://www.loc.gov/item/sanborn02775_005/.

210.8 NORA SPRINGS – The Iowa Northern Railway is located on the west side of the Shell Rock River while the City of Nora Springs is on the east side of the river. Nora Springs has a very interesting history related to its founding and naming. Four investors originally founded the town on May 23, 1857, naming it Woodstock. However, the town was not a success. Shortly thereafter, Edward P. Greeley offered to buy twenty acres of the town, build a store, and acquire and improve the existing mill if the town was renamed Elnora. The name Elnora came from a woman in Vermont whom Greeley hoped to marry. One of the community's founders countered with the name Springs, but finally the name Nora Springs was agreed upon.

The name Springs came about because there were more than 100 natural springs in the area, attracting both Indians and white settlers to the area. Some of the first settlers built a dam and flour mill using some of these springs. The mill later produced a fine patent flour by a process imported from Europe.

With the town named after this prospective bride, Greeley returned to Vermont to propose marriage, but was rejected by Elnora. Greeley was furious and never returned to Nora Springs, selling off his properties. The town was finally incorporated on September 17, 1874. The Rock Island assigned the station the code of "BN", but the Iowa Northern uses "NO". For the Milwaukee Road, their station was to the east. It was located east of Hawkeye Avenue and on the north side of the tracks. There were a Farmer's Elevator and Supply Company elevator (17,000 bushels and built in 1893) and coal sheds there.

Just to the north of the transfer track is the Nora Springs Elevator Track, located on the west side of the mainline. The Elevator Track straddles the county line and serves the Cartersville Elevator. This firm has elevator complexes at Nora Springs, Rockwell, and Mason City, Iowa.

The population of Nora Springs was 1369 in 2020. The community is the home of the annual Nora Springs Buffalo Days festival, scheduled for the last week of June. The festival includes a parade, entertainment, food vendors, a 5K run-walk, a softball tournament, a fireman's ball, and other events.

210.9 JEFFERSON HIGHWAY OVERPASS – The July 1922 issue of *Rock Island Magazine* announced that a steam ditcher outfit was "engaged in grading and excavating for the subway under our tracks at Nora Junction for the Jefferson highway. Contract for subway has been given to the Cedar Rapids Construction Company." The concrete bridge is still used to cross the highway, now known as West Drive.

The Jefferson Highway was a highway organized in 1915 as part of the National Auto Trail system. These roads were generally established by clubs and built by local farmers and communities along the route. Many later became national highways. This route connected New Orleans with Winnipeg in Canada. It was named for President Thomas Jefferson, who was responsible for the Louisiana Purchase. The road was also known as the Palm to Pine Highway.

211.1 COUNTY LINE – The county line is about where the Zinnia Avenue grade crossing is located. **Floyd County** is to the east while **Cerro Gordo County** is to the west.

Cerro Gordo County, in the early days of the state, was a part of Fayette County. The first white settlers came to the new county in 1851. As the population grew, a courthouse was established in Mason City in 1857. It was short-lived because in the summer of 1857, the county seat was moved to Livonia. A new courthouse was built there, and the county records and offices were soon located in this small town. This too was short-lived, because in April, 1858, Mason City won back the county seat in an election.

The county is named after the location of a battle in the Mexican War. At Cerro Gordo, General Winfield Scott defeated General Santa Ana of the Mexican army on April 18, 1847. The battle was significant because it opened the way for the United States to take Mexico City. The Spanish translation of Cerro Gordo is "fat hill." Near the west side of Cerro Gordo County is the site of the airplane crash that killed Buddy Holly, Ritchie Valens, and J. P. "The Big Bopper" Richardson on February 3, 1959.

Cerro Gordo County is somewhat unique for northern Iowa as it has a large number of manufacturing plants, generally around Mason City. Because of this, the county has a higher population than most counties in the area, with 43,127 residents in the 2020 census.

211.5 265TH STREET – The railroad passes under 265th Street/Business US-18, which connects Nora Springs with Mason City. The north switch for the siding that serves the Cartersville Elevator complex is under this bridge.

To the northeast is a series of large greenhouses, one of more than 70 growing stations across the country for Bonnie Plants. In 1918, Bonnie and Livingston Paulk began growing and selling vegetables at Union Springs, Alabama. Since then, the company has grown and now has growing facilities like this one scattered across the country.

213.4 STOFFER STORAGE – The Stoffer Storage Track is about 4200 feet long and is located on the west side of the mainline. It has been assigned the station code of "ST" by the Iowa Northern. Stoffer, built in 2007 as a partnership between the Iowa, Chicago &

Eastern Railroad (IC&E) and Iowa Northern Railway, is used as an interchange track between the two railroads. The IC&E provided the track material and the IANR built the track.

Stoffer was named for C. J. Stoffer, who had started a railroad career by working for the Rock Island Railroad in 1958. He worked for that railroad until 1980, holding jobs like telegrapher, station agent, train dispatcher, and chief train dispatcher. He helped to start up the Iowa Northern in 1981 and was its General Manager, and then president starting in 1986. He retired from the railroad in 1992.

Iowa Northern #3811 is shown here switching the south end of the Stoffer Storage Track in July 2010.

216.3 ROCK FALLS – Coming into Rock Falls from the south, the railroad passes Wilkinson Pioneer Park with its old through truss road bridge. From here to downtown Rock Falls, there is a series of parks and trails alongside the Shell Rock River to the east of the tracks.

The name Rock Falls was chosen by the railroad, since the original name of Shell Rock Falls was too similar to the existing town and station of Shell Rock. The original Shell Rock Falls name came from the local post office which opened in 1855, and the town was founded by Elijah Wiltfong in 1858. Wiltfong chose the location due to falls in the river, a requirement for a planned flour and sawmill. The population in the 1870 census was reported to be 221, the largest population ever recorded for the community.

When the railroad arrived in 1872, it hauled flour from the mill and ice from the river. Ice was quickly a major industry for Rock Falls. The same year, the railroad helped change the name of the community and post office to Rock Falls to avoid confusion with its station of Shell Rock, only 45 miles away. In 1880, ice dealer Robert Todd employed 100 men and 40 horses to cut and haul ice, requiring 1000 railroad cars to move it to market.

Rock Falls was incorporated on July 17, 1882. However, in 1888, the river flooded and destroyed much of the town, and Rock Falls never recovered. Despite a population of only 150 in the 2020 census, the community is still known as the City of Rock Falls. The town was always on the east side of the Shell Rock River, north of the tracks. To the south was the railroad and related facilities. Rock Falls didn't have a station code in the 1910 Rock Island station listing, but the Iowa Northern uses "FL". The 980-foot-long Rock Falls Elevator Track is located on the east side of the mainline. The Rock Falls Grain Company is a family-owned grain elevator based in Rock Falls, Iowa.

219.4 PLYMOUTH – This location is sometimes called Plymouth Junction. The City of Plymouth is located just to the northeast. The town was established by Thomas Tenney. This was his second attempt at founding a town named Plymouth. Plymouth was originally platted in 1858, located just north of Star Corner, a log cabin used as a stage coach and mail stop. A general store, post office, hotel, blacksmith shop and a stone schoolhouse were soon built, but little else happened. The new City of Plymouth was established on December 23, 1870, soon after the Chicago, Milwaukee & St. Paul Railway built through the site. Some believe that the name Plymouth came about due to the large glacial boulder found here, a boulder that reportedly reminded some of Plymouth Rock in Massachusetts. It was incorporated as a city on October 18, 1900.

The population of Plymouth was 375 in the 2020 census. The current city hall was built in 1925 to house the city's two 13,500-gallon water pressure storage tanks for the city water system. After a new fire department building was erected in 1958, the building was remodeled with library and council chambers, restrooms and a kitchen.

There is a connection to the Canadian Pacific line in the southeast quadrant of the diamond to allow CP trains to re-enter their tracks. That is the reason for this station. The CRIP didn't have a station code assigned in 1910, but the Iowa Northern uses "PL".

219.5 CPRS CROSSING – The Rock Island simply noted this location as CMSTP&P Crossing, but the name Plymouth Junction was also used. During the 1970s, Rock Island employee timetables identified this as a "railroad crossing not protected by interlocking."

Instead, there was an electric lock gate, lined against the Milwaukee Road. Now, the instructions state that the gate can be left lined in the position last used, and the crossing is protected by stop signs.

This former Milwaukee Road line runs between Austin, Minnesota, and Mason City, Iowa. The line was built in 1870 by the Mason City & Minnesota Railway as a part of a shortcut to the Twin Cities for the Milwaukee & St. Paul Railroad. As with other former Milwaukee Road routes, it has gone through a number of different owners and is today part of Canadian Pacific's Mason City to Twin Cities secondary line. This explains the Canadian Pacific trains that operate over the Iowa Northern between here and Nora Springs.

Just north of the diamond there was once a spur track into a North Iowa Co-op Elevator, used for the movement of fertilizers. A 65-car siding was also here into the 1960s.

221.7 COUNTY LINE – The county line is located at the grade crossing with 340th Street. **Cerro Gordo County** is to the south while to the north is **Worth County**. The north border of Worth County is Minnesota.

Worth County was created in 1851 and was attached to Mitchell County. It was named for Major General William Jenkins Worth, an officer in the War of 1812, Second Seminole War, Black Hawk War, and the Mexican-American War. During the Mexican-American War, Worth held a number of commands and is credited with personally climbing to the roof of the National Palace in Mexico City and taking down the Mexican flag, replacing it with the Stars and Stripes.

The first settler in the area arrived in 1853. A native of Norway, Gulbrand Mellem settled on the banks of the Shell Rock River, at the present-day site of Northwood. The main ethnic group to settle in Worth County were Norwegians. They were attracted to Worth County by the rich black soil, which is good for farming. The land was primarily gentle rolling prairie with an occasional oak grove, especially along the rivers and creeks. In 1857, the county was fully organized and the town of Northwood (north of Manly) became the county seat. As of the 2020 census, the population of Worth County was 7443.

223.8 REINDL STORAGE – The north switch of Reindl is at Broadway Street (Milepost 224.5) in Manly, while the south switch is at Quail Avenue (Milepost 223.0). This 7555-foot-long storage track is located to the west of the mainline and is designed to hold interchange trains between the Iowa Northern and Union Pacific railroads. It was built out of available material (used rail replaced by welded rail just north of Cedar Rapids and steel ties bought for the Butler project) to add immediate capacity during the flooding in 2008.

The name Reindl comes from the in-laws of the Sabin family. Many members of the Reindl family have lived in the area around Manly.

224.8 MANLY JUNCTION – This is a junction between the Iowa Northern and Union Pacific's mainline south out of Minneapolis, Minnesota. The Burlington, Cedar Rapids & Northern reached here in 1877, and the Rock Island used the Iowa Central northward to gain access to the Minneapolis & St.

Louis Railroad for Albert Lea and the Twin Cities. The result of this connection was the creation of an interesting St. Louis-Twin Cities route using CB&Q tracks south of Burlington, Iowa, and CRIP and M&St.L tracks north of there.

The name Manly comes from the name of a railroad contractor helping to build the line. The railroad has always called this location Manly Junction, and the first post office opened in 1877 using the name Manly Junction. The town of Manly was founded in 1877 when the BCR&N reached the Iowa Central Railway at this location. In 1883, the post office simplified its name to Manly. Manly was incorporated on November 19, 1898, and in 1912, the Rock Island made Manly a division point and built a yard, roundhouse, and other railroad buildings.

In 1913, Manly was very busy with three railroads – Rock Island, Minneapolis & St. Louis, and Chicago Great Western – with each having their own facilities. Just south of South Street, there were stockyards where the Iowa Northern locomotive #200 and Rock Island caboose #17054 are on display. There was a joint depot at the crossing of the railroads at the west end of Elmore Street. The depot was torn down in 1972, replaced by a small metal building. It was torn down by the CNW in 1985.

To the north were a number of other facilities, most in the Rock Island yard. Just east of the Main Street grade crossing is the Manly Junction Railroad Museum. The museum is in the former Oltman's Grocery store building at 101 E. Main Street. Dan Sabin, president of the Iowa Northern Railway, is a large supporter of the museum, which houses many Rock Island documents.

This sign marks the location of the Manly Junction Railroad Museum.

The 1967 Rock Island timetable called this CNW Crossing. The railroad uses a set of switches to cross over what is today Union Pacific's mainline south out of Minneapolis, Minnesota. The south switch is at Main Street. Less than two blocks further north is another switch where the Iowa Northern breaks off to the northwest. The Iowa Northern passes through the former Rock Island Manly Yard to gain access to the modern Manly Logistics Park and Manly Terminal.

Manly is a small community on US Highway 65, not far south of Minnesota. The original town was platted to the east of the railroads, with additions later added to the east and west. The population was 1256 in 2020.

The Iowa Northern Railway uses a short piece of Union Pacific track to reach its Manly Yard. During 2012, two UP locomotives pass through Manly on this mainline, temporarily delaying an Iowa Northern freight.

Manly's Railroad Park

On the south side of South Street (Iowa Highway 9) at Milepost 224.6 is a small park that features a former Iowa Northern locomotive and a Rock Island caboose. The locomotive is a GP-20 that was built by Electro-Motive Division in April 1962 as Southern Pacific #7233. Southern Pacific rebuilt the locomotive and renumbered it as #4101. It eventually became Iowa Northern #2000 and is now named "Arthur C. Sabin" and placed on display here in 2006.

The caboose is Chicago, Rock Island & Pacific #17054, built by International Car in 1964. The third attraction in the park is a life-size statue of a railroad conductor holding a lantern, selected by the Manly city council to represent Manly.

171

Thanks to the Iowa Northern Railway, this display of IANR #2000 and CRIP caboose #17054 can be found at Manly.

224.8 MANLY YARD – Early Rock Island documents used Milepost 224.8 as the location of Manly, sometimes called Manly Yard. During the 1950s the yard was shown to have a capacity of 798 freight cars. It was also shown to have a locomotive fueling facility, a train order station, and a train register station. In 1967, Manly was shown to be at Milepost 225.1.

The Rock Island and Iowa Northern both use "JU" as the station code for this facility. In Rock Island days, Manly was an important division point facility sporting a large yard and roundhouse. Shortly after the Rock's financial collapse, most of the yard tracks were removed. Today, Manly is again a major facility with enormous importance to the railroad. The Manly facility provides direct service to several customers, operates as a large transload terminal for numerous area customers, and serves as an interchange yard between Iowa Northern and Union Pacific.

The former Rock Island brick roundhouse, built in 1913, is today used for grain storage at the Viafield facility. The turntable is still there and was once used to turn locomotives when needed. The former CGW depot is also here with plans for its use by the Manly Junction Railroad Museum.

Currently at Manly, the IANR has three separate transload facilities. The most unique is Manly Terminal, an 82-acre liquids storage and transload facility developed in partnership with LB Transport, Inc. and Kenan Advantage Group for the purpose of supporting the distribution of ethanol and other bio-fuel related commodities. The terminal is reportedly the first-of-its-kind ethanol origin facility designed "to build efficiencies into ethanol transportation and trading. The terminal provides producers with a transload and storage site to consolidate ethanol gallons at origin. Manly Terminal customers can take advantage of the multiple rail connections of Iowa Northern to access markets quickly and economically." In plain English, the Manly Terminal began operations in October 2007 and "allows producers a common point to truck production to the facility where it can be staged, loaded into outbound railcars, and then assembled into unit trains for distribution throughout the United States." Why was this development important? Well, it was estimated that by the end of 2009, there would be 75 ethanol plants operating within a 275-mile radius of Manly. Union Pacific Distribution Services also operates a 20-acre facility here dedicated as a wind turbine component distribution center.

A second specialized transload facility is Manly Logistics Park, a 165-acre facility encompassing a nearly two-mile loop track with approximately 125 acres available for industrial development. It was developed as a transload yard for commodities such as caustic soda, sulfuric acid, corn oil, and methanol along with animal feeds and various other commodities. Part of the facility was built to specifically support the distribution of wind turbine components. Finally, there is the more generalized transload terminal, built with partner Halfman Family, LLC, that includes more than 160 acres of industrial development designed for warehousing, transloading and staging such products as denaturant, caustic soda, sulfuric acid, corn oil and methanol along with animal feeds or bagged products. As demand has increased, more transload facilities are being built.

For the regular railroad user, Iowa Northern's Manly Yard, located next to Manly Terminal and Manly Logistics Park, boasts a 700-car capacity. The IANR also has a small locomotive shed here that can be used for basic maintenance and to warm equipment in winter.

Over the past decade, the Iowa Northern has greatly expanded its facilities at Manly Yard, and now features miles of tracks like these.

The Customers at Manly Yard

While much of Manly Yard now consists of a series of transload terminals operated by the Iowa Northern, several rail customers have also located here. Heading north, trains of the Iowa Northern enter their large yard and pass a small car repair shop.

Next are the grain elevators of Viafield. Viafield is a member-owned ag cooperative in northern Iowa and southern Minnesota, dating back to the 1891 creation of the Farmers Cooperative Exchange of Rockford. Through the mergers of dozens of elevators and cooperatives, three organizations were formed: Progressive Ag, Farmers Co-op, and Northeast Iowa Co-op. In 2010, they merged to create Viafield. On September 12, 2023, the farmer members of Northern Country Cooperative and Viafield voted to merge the two agriculture retail companies. The new cooperative began conducting unified business effective February 1, 2024. Viafield is a large part of the 5,000,000 bushels of grain storage capacity at Manly.

On the north side of the Viafield facility is the old Rock Island roundhouse and turntable. The roundhouse has been used for storage by Viafield for many years. To the north of the rail yard are the storage tanks and warehouses of the various transload and storage facilities.

North of 380th Street and sitting on five acres is Sukup Manufacturing. This steel receiving facility was built in 2015 to handle steel for the Sukup Manufacturing Company. The company was founded in 1963 to manufacture grain stirring machines for storage bins. In 2001, Sukup began manufacturing grain bins. Today, Sukup Manufacturing is the world's largest family-owned and operated manufacturer of grain storage, grain drying and handling equipment, and steel buildings. North of Sukup is a large loop track to the west of the Union Pacific mainline. This track goes as far as 380th Street.

In August 2011, IANR #3806 was switching wind turbine parts at Manly Yard at the north end of the Iowa Northern Railway.

226.7 UNION PACIFIC SWITCH AT NORTH MANLY
– This is the primary access point for many Union Pacific trains as they handle interchange traffic with the Iowa Northern. It is located at 380th Street.

Waterloo to Oelwein
Oelwein Subdivision

Although the Iowa Northern abandoned a few branch lines over the years, they also expanded some when they acquired the operating rights over their Oelwein Subdivision. This route has a history of changing ownership, operating leases, and new customers, which can make its story a bit complex.

After Union Pacific acquired the Chicago & North Western on June 23, 1995, the line between Waterloo and Oelwein stuck out like a sore thumb. Except for the shippers in the Waterloo area, Union Pacific saw little value in the line. Transco Railway Products, located in the old Chicago Great Western shops at Oelwein, became concerned that they might lose their rail access. In October 2003, Transco finalized the purchase of the rail line between Dewar (just outside of Waterloo) and Oelwein. Transco named the line the D&W Railroad, the initials of two Transco employees who had lost their lives on the job. Transco then leased the line to IANR, which maintained, marketed, and provided train service between Waterloo and Oelwein.

On May 18, 2020, Iowa Northern sent a finalized proposal to the Surface Transportation Board to acquire from D&W Railroad approximately 23.40 miles of rail line. This included the track from Milepost 332.0 (Dewar) to Milepost 354.5 (end of line), which included "The Main Line", which was the easterly rail line adjacent to the Oelwein Yard. Other smaller parts were included in the sale, including the rail line from Milepost 245.58 to Milepost 245.0 at Oelwein, and 0.32 miles of wye track that connected the east-west mainline and the north-south mainline. The

Iowa Northern Railway Company officially acquired the trackage that June.

This line was originally part of the Chicago Great Western network of rail lines. The Chicago Great Western Railway was a Class I railroad that linked Chicago, Minneapolis, Omaha, and Kansas City. In 1854, the Legislature of the Territory of Minnesota had chartered the Minnesota & Northwestern Railroad to be built between Lake Superior, Minneapolis, and Dubuque, Iowa. However, it stayed dormant until purchased by Alpheus Beede Stickney and another investor in 1883. Immediately, the railroad began building, and by 1886 had constructed a line between St. Paul, Minnesota, and Dubuque, Iowa, via Oelwein.

The 26.49-mile-long line between Oelwein and Waterloo was built in 1887 as part of a plan to acquire a route to Kansas City, building track connecting several existing railroads which were also acquired. The railroad changed its name to the Chicago, St. Paul & Kansas City Railway Company on June 10, 1886, and was then sold to the Chicago Great Western Railway Company (incorporated on January 16, 1892) on September 7, 1893. By this time, the CGW had reached Chicago and Omaha.

Through mergers and new construction, the railroad, renamed Chicago Great Western after 1892, quickly became a multi-state carrier. One of the last Class I railroads to be built, it competed against several other more well-established railroads in the same territory, and developed a corporate culture of innovation and efficiency to survive. With all of these lines meeting here, Oelwein became the hub of the railroad, and its main locomotive repair shops were soon located here.

The railroad had two common nicknames. First, many knew it as the *Corn Belt Route* because of its operating area in the midwestern United States. Additionally, the railroad was sometimes called the *Lucky Strike Road* due to the similarity in design between the herald of the CGW and the logo used for Lucky Strike cigarettes.

The Chicago Great Western Railroad merged with the Chicago & North Western Railway in 1968, which abandoned most of the CGW's trackage. The Chicago & North Western was purchased by the Union Pacific Railroad in 1995. Today, this line is the longest piece of CGW trackage left in Iowa. For the Iowa Northern, this is the Oelwein Subdivision. It is generally served by trains out of Waterloo, which operate over several miles of Union Pacific track through downtown Waterloo, Iowa.

Union Pacific Waterloo Industrial Lead

This railroad was originally the Chicago, St. Paul & Kansas City Railway (CSP&KC), the third railroad to reach Waterloo. The CSP&KC started as the Minnesota & North Western (M&NW), which built a line south from St. Paul, Minnesota, to Dubuque, Iowa, by 1884. The M&NW was acquired by the CSP&KC in 1887, and the new railroad built lines west to Omaha, Nebraska, south to St. Joseph, Missouri, and east to Chicago, Illinois, by 1892. The construction caused the railroad to fail, and it was reorganized as part of the Chicago Great Western (CGW) in 1893. During the early 1900s, the railroad continued to face financial difficulties before being acquired by the Chicago & North Western Railway in 1968. Soon, most of the former CGW routes were abandoned. The C&NW was purchased by Union Pacific in April 1995, explaining this isolated piece of UP track.

Union Pacific timetables show this short stretch of track to be the Waterloo Industrial Lead, and it is used to serve a small number of shippers on the east side of Waterloo, Iowa. UP based a crew here to handle local switching, and then had the Iowa Northern handle the cars to Union Pacific mainlines at either Cedar Rapids or Manly. However, in 2019, Union Pacific leased the operation to the Iowa Northern, ending their direct presence in Waterloo. According to the Notice published in the March 20, 2019, *Federal Register*, the Iowa Northern would "lease from Union Pacific Railroad Company (UP) and operate approximately 6.9 miles of rail line in Black Hawk County, Iowa, known as the Waterloo Industrial Line (the Line). The Line is located between milepost 325.1 and milepost 332.0 and includes a rail yard located at approximately milepost 326.5 and certain side tracks located at approximately milepost 329.0 and milepost 331.5." The Notice stated that there was an interchange commitment in the lease that "will require IANR to pay additional charges to UP for carloads that originate or terminate on the Line that are not interchanged with UP." Iowa Northern operations began April 3, 2019, and some improvements in track and bridge conditions were expected as operations changed.

325.1 IANR CONNECTION – This is the location of the Iowa Northern-Union Pacific junction shown in the *Union Pacific Iowa Area Timetable #4*, dated October 10, 2011. It is at the west end of the Cedar River bridge.

325.1 CEDAR RIVER BRIDGE – This 730-foot long, eight-span through plate girder bridge, was built in 1901 by the American Bridge Company of New York. It was partially swept away by high floodwaters on the Cedar River on Tuesday, June 10, 2008. Spans 5 through 8 fell into the river. The issue in rebuilding the bridge was that while Union Pacific owns the bridge, it is the Iowa Northern that uses it. While plans were made to rebuild the bridge, negotiations were conducted to determine where the funds were going to come from, and both railroads waited for the Corps of Engineers to sign off on the design phase. This situation caused big headaches for rail customers across eastern Iowa. Everything from grain to ethanol to John Deere tractors had to be detoured for hundreds of miles. For example, much of the traffic had to go north to Manly – then back south to Nevada, Iowa – then east to Cedar Rapids. This was a detour of around 300 miles for nearly two-thirds of the rail company's business. As Dan Sabin, Iowa Northern President said at the time, "It's tremendously expensive."

During the reconstruction of the bridge, spans 5 through 8 were heat straightened and reinstalled, piers 5-7 were rebuilt, and all new decking and rail was installed. On September 28, 2009, more than a year after the flood, the new bridge was commemorated and the first IANR train crossed it on October 6, 2009.

Heading northeast, locomotive engineers must stay on their toes, or at least the horn, as there are streets and trails throughout the next five city blocks of downtown Waterloo.

325.3 CHICAGO GREAT WESTERN RAILROAD FREIGHT DEPOT – To the north of the tracks is the University of Northern Iowa Center for Urban Education (UNI-CUE), housed in the former Waterloo freight depot of the Chicago Great Western. This 1903 structure is listed on the National Register of Historic Places (1997), and is described as a two-story concrete block freight depot built on a rough limestone foundation. The building features round arch freight doors and a simple wood cornice. There is also a concrete block addition on the southwest side. This was the second freight house built by the railroad, which was also the first to build a depot downtown.

Illinois Central once had an interchange connection here. The track headed south along the Cedar River, and then looped back east to connect to the mainline. Most of this grade is still visible.

326.0 BRIDGE OVER CANADIAN NATIONAL – At one time, this bridge carried two tracks across the Illinois Central. Today, this is the Waterloo Subdivision of the Canadian National. It is part of the route from Chicago west to Fort Dodge, where the line splits to reach Council Bluffs and Sioux Falls, both in Iowa. Below is the east end of Canadian National's Waterloo Yard. At the west end of the yard is the old roundhouse and turntable.

326.1 WATERLOO – Some sources show this to be Lynden Avenue Junction. It is a junction between Union Pacific and Canadian National, used by the Iowa Northern as a part of their Waterloo to Cedar Falls route. Union Pacific owns the tracks from here east to milepost 332.0. It is known as the Waterloo Industrial Lead.

326.2 LINDEN YARD – Is it Linden or Lynden? Both spellings have been in print over the years. The modern spelling tends to be Linden. There are about five yard tracks plus a siding here, which carries Union Pacific Station Letter NW001. The track to the east is used by Iowa Northern employees to prepare flatcars for loading by John Deere.

According to an article in the April 2008 *Railroads Illustrated*, "UP bases a switch crew out of the former CGW yard, in northeast Waterloo, to serve a contingent of customers in the area, like farm tractor and implement manufacturer John Deere; Tyson Foods, formerly Iowa Beef Processors; and Kinder Morgan Terminals, a fertilizer warehouse and distribution center." Lynden Yard and a few miles of track to the east are all of the railroad in Waterloo that Union Pacific owns. Therefore, in the past, Iowa Northern handled traffic in and out of Waterloo for Union Pacific, mainly with the UP at Cedar Rapids.

The yard is all located west of the railroad bridge over Idaho Street. In 2019, the Iowa Northern Railway assumed the switching responsibilities for Union Pacific, simplifying the railroad operations in and around Linden Yard.

In 2010, Union Pacific still switched Linden Yard, at the time using UP Y657.

327.0 WATERLOO, CEDAR FALLS & NORTHERN UNDERPASS – Look for the high voltage line overhead. Below is the former grade of this railroad. In 1895, the Waterloo & Cedar Falls Rapid Transit Company (W&CFRT) was created to build an electric rail system in the Waterloo-Cedar Falls area. By 1897, a line connected the two towns. The company was reorganized in 1904 as the Waterloo, Cedar Falls & Northern Railway (WCF&N). Connecting with the Chicago Great Western allowed the line to also handle carload freight, an important part of the railroad's operation. The WCF&N even operated on the Chicago Great Western using trackage rights. The WCF&N built south toward Cedar Rapids starting in 1912, creating this grade.

The Illinois Central and Rock Island railroads bought the WCF&N in 1956, creating the Waterloo Railroad. Electric service ended in 1957 and trains used a fleet of small diesel locomotives. The Rock Island sold its part of the company in 1968, and the IC immediately began abandoning most of the Waterloo Railroad. The trackage around Waterloo was sold to the Chicago, Central & Pacific Railroad in late 1985, then reacquired by IC in 1996. Canadian National bought the IC in 1999. Much of the route south of here is the Cedar Valley Nature Trail.

329.5 ARMOUR – This station is located around the grade crossing with North Elk Run Road. This is Union Pacific Station Letter NW004. The reason that Union Pacific kept control of the line to here is rather obvious. Look to the north and you will see the large John Deere Waterloo Works complex. This is their Tractor Cab & Assembly Operations (TCAO). Tractor assembly in the Waterloo area has a long history, including the Waterloo Gasoline Traction Engine Company, which manufactured the Waterloo Boy tractor. John Deere acquired the company in 1918. This modern facility replaced the original John Deere tractor factory building in downtown Waterloo, which now houses the John Deere Tractor & Engine Museum. A number of the tractors are loaded on flatcars and shipped by rail, especially those for export. Union Pacific historically moved them to Waterloo, and then the Iowa Northern on to Cedar Rapids. At Cedar Rapids, the tractors generally are handed back to Union Pacific, which moves them east or west. With Iowa Northern now handling the switching here, the move to Cedar Rapids has been simplified.

To the south is Tyson Fresh Meats, the former IBP (Iowa Beef Packers) plant. Waterloo has long had a history with the meat industry. In 1891, the Rath Packing Company, a family-owned meat company, opened a pork processing plant in Waterloo. Thanks to the demand for canned meats during World Wars I and II, Rath Packing became one of the nation's biggest meatpackers. It became known for its Black Hawk Bacon and vacuum-cooked Tend'r Ham. During the 1960s, Iowa Beef Packers used the assembly line concept to butcher beef, and built the world's largest hog-slaughtering plant in Waterloo during the late 1980s, just a few years after Rath Packing had closed due to the inability to compete in the changing meat market.

All was not well though. During the 1960s, IBP went through several legal battles with unions. Several times the employees went on strike, often with violent results. For example, before a late 1960s strike ended on April 13, 1970, there had been one death, 56 bombings, more than 20 shootings, numerous tire slashings, death threats, extensive property damage, and the fire-bombing of the home of an IBP vice president. Despite this, IBP became the largest beef producer in the world. About the same time, a co-founder of IBP was working a scheme to enter new markets and settle problems with unions. The scheme involved a deal with a meat broker with underworld ties, who obtained meat contracts with New York supermarket chains. The broker was paid almost $1 million on all beef sold within 125 miles of downtown Manhattan over a period of about 30 months. This money was then used to pay off union officials and supermarket executives. The firm was indicted in March 1973, but eventually was found guilty of only two charges and was fined only $7000, based upon the finding that IBP "had been victimized by the corruption of New York's meat business." In 1990, IBP opened a new plant in Waterloo, Iowa. After going through several ownerships and management teams, Tyson Foods acquired the company in 2001 and changed the name in 2003. This plant primarily serves as a pork processing plant.

Tyson Foods is big, producing 20% of the chicken, beef, and pork in the United States. Tyson Foods started in 1931 when John W. Tyson moved to Springdale, Arkansas, and to feed his family, began buying chickens locally and selling them across the Midwest. The business grew rapidly during World War II as poultry was one of the few foods not rationed, and Tyson moved into chicken production. The company was incorporated in 1947 as Tyson Feed and Hatchery, Inc. During the late 1950s, the company built its first processing plant, meaning that it raised, processed and sold poultry, one of the first firms to control the entire process.

In 1963, Tyson's Foods went public, allowing it to continue to expand. The name became Tyson Foods in 1972, and other product lines were added throughout the 1980s. By 1990, Tyson Foods was the world's largest fully-integrated producer, processor, and marketer of poultry-based food products, and was quickly expanding its international market. Thanks to further expansion and several acquisitions, Tyson became the world's largest processor and marketer of chicken, beef, and pork by 2001. Since then, the company has continued to expand and the product names on the side of their trailers will surprise almost anyone.

A Watco bulk reload terminal, known as the Waterloo Blackhawk Transload Terminal, is located just east of Tyson. The facility was operated by Midwest Bulk Services, and then Kinder Morgan Terminals. The facility has typically accepted delivery of 100-car unit potash trains and stored the product until it was required. Approximately 80,000 tons of potash was received annually via unit trains that are brought in through the UP/IANR connection at Manly.

During November 2016, Watco acquired 20 domestic bulk terminals from Kinder Morgan, including this one. Watco states that their Waterloo Blackhawk Transload Terminal handles any commodity, but they primarily handle steel bar, potash, palletized steel round stock, and fertilizer. The site has 115 railcar spots, 32,000 tons of inside storage capacity, and 20,000 tons of outdoor but covered storage. They can handle unit trains with their own switch engine. Kinder Morgan also had their switch locomotives, a former Boston & Maine SW9 and an ex-Baltimore & Ohio Chicago Terminal SW1.

330.2 ELK RUN CREEK BRIDGE – Elk Run Creek forms just north of this bridge from two branches. The west branch forms in open farmland less than ten miles to the north. The railroad follows the east branch to Dewar, near where it starts. The Elk Run Creek flows south into the Cedar River near Evansdale, Iowa.

For years, this bridge was a mix of bridge types. On the west end were three open deck timber spans. In the center of the bridge, set on four concrete piers, were three I-beam ballast deck spans. On the east end were eight timber ballast deck spans set on timber piles. During the past few years, the Iowa Northern has worked on this structure as part of a plan to increase its tonnage rating.

331.6 DEWAR – Dewar was originally named Emert in October 1880 after the original landowners John and Elizabeth Emert. However, there was some confusion with mail going to Emmetsburg, Iowa. Reportedly, the town was renamed DeWar after a railroad surveyor. A post office opened on October 25, 1887, and the town was platted in 1888. However, Dewar is unincorporated.

Dewar, as it is spelled now, carries the Union Pacific Station Letter NW007. The AgVantage grain elevator complex is located on the north side of the subdivision's mainline. AgVantage FS dates its history back to 1931, organized as a co-operative. On September 1, 2009, AgVantage FS became a retail division of GROWMARK, with its main office located in Waverly, Iowa. The organization operates in Iowa and Minnesota.

In 1910, there were stock yards and an elevator on the north side of the tracks. On the east edge of town were other businesses such as a creamery, an implements dealer, and a meat market. The depot was on the south side of the tracks at the end of Stickney Street, where the dirt grade crossing is today. Heading east, the railroad crosses the Pleasant Valley Creek Branch of the Elk Run, as it was known in 1910. It is the East Branch of the Elk Run that the railroad has been following eastward for the last several miles.

332.0 PROPERTY LIMITS – West of here the tracks are still owned by Union Pacific, but operated by Iowa Northern. East of here, the tracks are owned by the Iowa Northern Railway. Heading east, the tracks begin to climb, at times up to 1.0%, to the top of the hill at Milepost 335.

When Union Pacific proposed to abandon the line to Oelwein, Transco Railway Products created the D&W Railroad in 2002 to acquire the line and preserve its service. According to a number of sources, the name D&W came about to honor two Transco employees – Dan and Woody – who lost their lives in a tragic accident in Oelwein. The purchase resulted in the D&W Railroad owning:

[1] Track between milepost 332.0 at Dewar, IA, and milepost 354.3 at Oelwein, IA;

[2] Track between milepost 245.58 and milepost 245.0 at Oelwein;

[3] 0.32 miles of wye track at Oelwein; and

[4] Trackage rights over Union Pacific Railroad Company's track between milepost 332.0 at

Dewar and milepost 326.2 at Linden Street, Waterloo, IA.

In 2003, the Iowa Northern Railway reached an agreement to lease the operating rights on the D&W Railroad, with a statement from the time indicating that the IANR intended to consummate the transaction on or soon after September 26, 2003.

An interesting ownership issue came about in 2006 when Hawkeye Renewables became part owner of the line from Dewer to just outside Fairbank. This was part of the agreement to locate the plant at Fairbank. When Hawkeye sold out to Flint Hills Resources Renewables on February 17, 2011, the part ownership was relinquished back to Transco. During June 2020, the Iowa Northern Railway Company purchased the railroad assets of the D&W Railroad between here and the end of track at Oelwein, Iowa.

336.1 DUNKERTON – James and John Dunkerton claimed land in this area in 1853, and eventually a small community called Lesterton developed. John Dunkerton died in 1854 and James took over the farm. When talk of a railroad building through the area started, James Dunkerton sold a portion of his land to the railroad, and established the town of Dunkerton in 1886, the same year the post office opened. The City of Dunkerton was incorporated on March 18, 1899. A 1910 map shows railroad stock yards, an elevator, and a creamery in Dunkerton. The depot was to the south of the tracks between Main and Lincoln Streets, where the large building stands today. The town never grew much, and its population in 2020 was 842.

Today, there are a number of sidings and business tracks at Dunkerton, including an elevator track and a fertilizer track to the south at Dunkerton Street. The company wasn't shipping by rail when the Iowa Northern began operating this line, but has now become a major shipper. The Dunkerton Cooperative has added additional fertilizer capacity and a second loadout track, all designed to use the railroad to move grain to multiple markets.

336.2 CRANE CREEK BRIDGE – This bridge has 14 wood spans, one I-beam span, and then two more wood spans, going from east to west. Crane Creek runs along the northeast side of Dunkerton. It starts about fifteen miles northwest of here, and flows to the southeast until it enters the Wapsipinicon River several miles east of here.

338.8 BRIDGE – This 11-span timber trestle crosses a former channel of the Wapsipinicon River. To the southeast is the Bruggeman Wildlife Area, which contains 359 acres of primarily floodplain timber on the Wapsipinicon River. The park includes the opportunity to hike, fish, hunt, cross country ski, and canoe on the Wapsipinicon River.

339.0 WAPSIPINICON RIVER BRIDGE – This bridge consists of two deck plate girder spans. Locals generally just use the term Wapsi River. The name of the river in the Ojibwe language is Waabizipin-ikaan-ziibi ("river abundant in swan-potatoes"), on account of the large quantity of arrowheads or wild artichokes, known as "swan-potatoes" (waabizipini-in, singular waabizipin), once found near its banks.

Trains heading east begin a fairly steady climb, generally between 0.4% and 0.8%.

341.6 BUCK CREEK BRIDGE – This bridge has seven timber spans on each end with an I-beam span in the center. Buck Creek starts about thirty miles to the north and flows southward, generally about three miles east of the Wapsipinicon River, until the two merge about seven miles south of here. Heading west from here, the railroad grade is 1.25%, going east it is 0.8%.

342.8 COUNTY LINE – The county line is located at the farm crossing just west of the Baxter Avenue road crossing. To the west is **Black Hawk County** while to the east it is **Buchanan County**.

Black Hawk County was created in 1843 and named for the Sac war leader who lost the war that bears his name (and who never set foot in the area named for him). However, with no permanent population, the county was first administered by Delaware County (1843-1845), then Benton County (1845-1851), and then Buchanan County (1851-1853). In 1853, Black Hawk County was allowed to organize its own government and elect officers, making Waterloo its county seat.

Meanwhile, in 1845, at a ford in the river that had long been used by Indian tribes, settlers George and Mary Hanna created the community of Prairie Rapids that attracted other settlers. At about the same time, a mill was built nearby at what was called Sturgis Falls. Thus, Sturgis Falls and Prairie Rapids, later to be renamed Cedar Falls and Waterloo, became in 1845 the first settlements in Black Hawk County, and between them at the end of the year they boasted the county's entire white population of thirteen pioneers.

Surrounded by some of the richest farmland to be found anywhere on the globe, the cities of Black Hawk County became important centers for the agricultural community. Despite a brief period of high water, which allowed the steamboat *Black Hawk* to make twenty-four round trips between Cedar Rapids and Waterloo in 1859, the Cedar River was not destined to provide a transportation advantage. Thus, it was the arrival of railroads that opened up the nation's markets to the farms of Black Hawk County.

Today, Black Hawk County is Iowa's fifth-most populous county, with 131,144 residents reported in the 2020 census.

The **Buchanan County** website explains a bit about the county's history. "An act approved by the Wisconsin Territorial Legislature on December 21, 1837, established boundaries for the county lying west of Delaware County and running to the western edge of the territory at the Missouri River. The county was in all other respects a part of Dubuque County, but this was the first step towards the growth of a new county, Buchanan County. It is said S. P. Stoughton, a strong Democrat, suggested naming the county after Senator (later president) James Buchanan, for Buchanan was instrumental in the acquisition of the Wisconsin Territory. In 1843 the county was reduced to its present limits of 571 square miles or 365,627 acres."

Buchanan County was not open for settlement until 1842. In February of that year, William Bennett came to the area now known as Quasqueton and built a cabin. The first county election was in August of 1847. Independence is the county seat, and in the 2020 census, the population was 20,565.

343.2 LITTLE WAPSIPINICON RIVER BRIDGE – This bridge uses two deck plate girder spans to cross the river. The two rivers with the name Wapsipinicon start to the north and flow southward, always within just a few miles of each other. The Little Wapsipinicon flows southward and into the Wapsipinicon River near Littleton, Iowa.

343.8 FAIRBANK – Fairbank was named for the grandmother of C. W. Bacon, who along with F. J. Everett, founded the Village of Fairbank in 1854. The post office opened the same year with Bacon as the postmaster. Everett and Bacon soon opened a sawmill on the Little Wapsipinicon River, producing lumber for area construction. The City of Fairbank was incorporated in October 1891, caused by the community's growth following the construction of the railroad. The railroad passes through the south side of town, which had a population of 1111 in 2020.

On the east side of Fairbank is a significant shipper for the Iowa Northern. Milepost 343.8 is the west end of the facility, located just east of Main Street. The siding to the south passes a series of small warehouses and barns that were once full of rail shippers. It then connects with tracks into the POET Fairbank Bioprocessing plant. This was the Fairbank Ethanol Plant, Hawkeye Renewables second ethanol plant. Construction of the 115 million gallon-per-year plant was completed in May of 2006. However, Hawkeye Renewables filed for Chapter 11 bankruptcy in December 2009, and sold the plant in 2011 to Flint Hills Resources Renewables. POET acquired the Fairbank plant on June 1, 2021, and it now produces 132 million gallons of bioethanol annually. POET Bioprocessing receives a large percentage of its inbound corn by rail, coming from all of IANR's online elevators, and some offline sources as well.

At the east end of the bioprocessing plant there is a crossover between the siding and mainline. The two tracks continue to the east to a switch located a short distance west of Unicorn Road (Milepost 345.5).

345.5 COUNTY LINE – The county line is located just east of the east switch of the Flint Hills ethanol plant. **Buchanan County** is to the south and **Fayette County** is to the north. For several years, there was an office container to the south, used by crews to get their train orders when starting here. This small office was installed during the 2008 flooding to provide a base for train operations on the line.

Fayette County was founded in 1837 by the Wisconsin Territory, which controlled the land at the time. It was named after Gilbert du Motier, Marquis de La Fayette, a French general and politician, who came to America in 1777 in order to fight in the Revolutionary War, and who was named Major General of the Continental Army. The county was finally organized in 1850. The area between Fairbank and Oelwein is made up of several small Amish communities. On "Market Days", visitors are welcome. You can shop at the bakeries, woodworking shops and general store.

The county seat of Fayette County is West Union, although Oelwein is the county's largest city. The county's population in 2020 was 19,509, part of a downward trend since the county reached its population peak of 29,251 in 1920.

350.1 OTTER CREEK BRIDGE – This is the largest wooded area along the entire Oelwein Subdivision. The Otter Creek Bridge consists of a deck plate girder with a center pier. Otter Creek drains the area immediately to the north of Oelwein, and flows southward before entering the Wapsipinicon River. The Yard Limits for Oelwein start just west of the bridge.

351.0 OELWEIN – Today, Oelwein is the largest community in Fayette County with about 6000 people calling Oelwein home. The town of Oelwein was originally laid out in a cornfield purchased from G. A. Oelwein in 1872. The townsite was developed due to the construction of the Burlington, Cedar Rapids & Minnesota Railroad through the area, which built north from Linn Junction near Cedar Rapids. The Rock Island abandoned the route in 1976.

The Minnesota & Northwestern (M&NW) built their line from St. Paul to Oelwein in 1886. At Oelwein, the M&NW connected with another railroad, the Dubuque & Dakota. During the late 1870s, the Dubuque & Dakota (D&D) built a line from Dubuque west to Oelwein and on west through Clarksville, Iowa. The Minnesota & Northwestern purchased the D&D in 1887, giving it a St. Paul to Dubuque mainline. The M&NW was acquired by the Chicago, St. Paul & Kansas City Railroad in 1887. By 1890, the railroad had built a line from Oelwein to the southwest through Des Moines to Kansas City, and another line to Omaha, Nebraska, by 1903. On January 11, 1892, the Chicago Great Western was created, with four lines joining at Oelwein.

Oelwein is considered the "Hub City" of northeast Iowa. This nickname came about due to the fact that Oelwein was the intersecting hub of the Chicago Great Western Railway with four main lines radiating from Oelwein, stretching to Chicago, the Twin Cities, Omaha, and Kansas City. In 1904, the railroad decided to move many of their facilities to Oelwein. Here, a large switching yard and car and locomotive shops once employed 1200 people. The mammoth facility was said to have inspired Walter Chrysler, who worked as the supervisor of the shops between 1904 and 1910. The CGW was acquired by the Chicago & North Western Railway in 1968. The CNW started abandoning tracks out of Oelwein in 1981 when the route east to Dubuque was removed. In the same year, the route to the northwest was abandoned from Oelwein to Randolph, Minnesota. The line west through Shell Rock was abandoned in 1986.

Not only were the various routes abandoned, but the shops at Oelwein were shut down. Transco acquired the car shop in 1969, the year after CNW acquired the CGW. Currently, Transco employs up to 100 people and utilizes a pair of SW1 switchers to move cars about the repair areas. Transco Railway Products is part of the Marmon Railcar Repair Group, which also includes Procor and UTLX, making Marmon the largest railcar repair network in North America. The Transco shops became a part of Marmon in 2019 and offer railcar repair, railcar parts, and railcar maintenance services.

The railroad brought many jobs to Oelwein. In 1895, the population had increased to 1928, leading to the incorporation of Oelwein in 1897. The population reached 5000 in 1900, peaked at about 7000 in 2000 before dropping to 6415 in 2010, and then 5920 in 2020.

This view from 2011 shows just a small part of the former Chicago Great Western shops at Oelwein.

In 1914, the Chicago Great Western had their Oelwein depot immediately south of the intersection of Charles Street and Third Avenue. This is about where the Oelwein Fire Department now stands, north of the Hub City Heritage Railway Museum complex. *Sanborn Fire Insurance Map from Oelwein, Fayette County, Iowa.* Sanborn Map Company, Feb, 1914. Map. Retrieved from the Library of Congress, https://www.loc.gov/item/sanborn02782_005/.

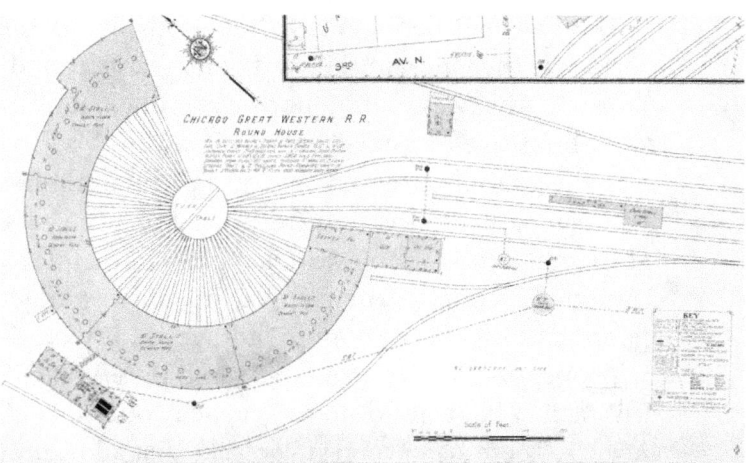

In 1914, Sanborn produced a series of maps about Oelwein that included this drawing of the 40-stall Chicago Great Western Roundhouse. Much of this building still exists and is used by Transco Railway Products. *Sanborn Fire Insurance Map from Oelwein, Fayette County, Iowa.* Sanborn Map Company, February 1914. Map. Retrieved from the Library of Congress, https://www.loc.gov/item/sanborn02782_005/.

The Railroad Today

Coming into Oelwein from the west, a wye track breaks off at Milepost 350.7. The mainline between Chicago and St. Paul consisted of a large number of tracks. On the east leg of the wye was a large stock yard complex. In 1914, maps showed that there was not a north wye track, but what is now the mainline was built later.

At the north switch and to the west were the CGW machine shop and car shop. There were also a number of other shop facilities including a passenger coach shop, car painting shops, blacksmith shop, planing mill, wheel shop, and a number of warehouses.

The Oelwein depot was to the east. Just to the north was the Oelwein rail yard with a large round-house to the west. The shops are gone, but the roundhouse still stands. Transco Railway Products uses the roundhouse and several nearby buildings for car repair, and the railyard is used to store cars. At the north end of the yard is a new shop built by Transco. The tracks extend approximately two miles before ending at a new grain storage facility originally operated by Oelwein Grain, and then Viafield. This facility has a grain storage capacity of 2,700,000 bushels. There are several stub tracks that allow unit train loading. The Iowa Northern serves these industries as needed.

The north-south Rock Island line ran through what is today Rock Island Road, also known as Iowa Highway 150. It crossed the CGW near the east switch of the wye. The right-of-way north of downtown passes behind a series of businesses and can still be found in a number of locations.

Hub City Heritage Railway Museum

Of interest to rail historians at Oelwein is the Hub City Heritage Railway Museum. Artifacts are housed in the former CGW passenger station and yard office building, including the yardmaster's high tower. Hub City Heritage was formed in early 1987 and opened the railway museum on June 14, 1987. In 1989, the museum acquired the Railway Express building. The Railway Express building was originally the home of Wells Fargo and Company Express in 1912. In 1918, the structure was acquired by the American Express Company and in 1930 became the Railway Express Agency. Through this shipping agency many things were transported, including live animals, furniture and machinery. Many horses were shipped from this area.

Since then, Hub City Heritage has acquired the two-story yard office building and the 75-foot dispatchers' tower, which is the last of the CGW dispatcher towers. The museum also displays a great deal of equipment, including a Chicago, St Paul Minneapolis & Omaha SW1 #55 built in 1940, a Chicago Great Western EMD FP7, a 40' CGW steel box car built in 1944, a CGW covered hopper, Rock Island caboose #17958 built in 1914, CGW #637 bay window caboose built in 1963, and Minnesota Transfer #62 S1 diesel built in 1941.

CRIP Caboose #17958 is part of the collection of railroad equipment at the Hub City Heritage Railway Museum at Oelwein.

Nora Junction/Plymouth Junction to Garner
Trackage Rights on Canadian Pacific

When the Iowa Northern applied "to operate approximately 27.83 miles of rail line owned by Union Pacific Railroad Company (UP), referred to as the Forest City Line," the railroad also applied and received trackage rights over three separate lines of the "Dakota, Minnesota & Eastern Railroad Corporation d/b/a Canadian Pacific." These trackage rights over the Canadian Pacific U.S. East Region were required to reach Garner to access their Belmond to Forest City line.

In the May 27, 2011, *Federal Register*, the Surface Transportation Board published a notice that described these trackage rights. They include the following three route segments, with each of them being described individually.

[1] Milepost 107.3 near Nora Junction and Milepost 116.7 at the connection with CP's Mason City Subdivision.

[2] Milepost 7.9 near Plymouth Junction and Milepost 116.7 at the connection with CP's Mason City Subdivision.

[3] Milepost 116.7 at the connection with CP's Mason City Subdivision and Milepost 137.5 near Garner.

On April 14, 2023, Canadian Pacific (CP) and Kansas City Southern (KCS) merged to create the only single-line railway connecting Canada, the U.S. and Mexico. The new merged railroad uses the name Canadian Pacific Kansas City Limited (CPKC). However, CP or Canadian Pacific will still be used in the description of these trackage rights.

Nora Springs to Mason City
Canadian Pacific Mason City Subdivision

The McGregor & Sioux City Railway, incorporated January 23, 1868, built into Nora Springs from the east in 1869. Renamed the McGregor & Missouri River Railway, the railway built further west in 1870 using available land grants. It was soon absorbed by its parent company, the Milwaukee & St. Paul, which became the Chicago, Milwaukee & St. Paul Railway (CM&StP) in 1874. The CM&StP declared bankruptcy in 1925 and reorganized as the Chicago, Milwaukee, St. Paul & Pacific Railroad in 1928.

After the failure of the Milwaukee Road on December 19, 1977, its third bankruptcy in 42 years, the line was acquired by the Soo Line, a part of Canadian Pacific, on January 1, 1986. In 1997, the I&M Rail Link (IMRL) acquired this line from Canadian Pacific/Soo Line. After several years of economic problems, the Dakota, Minnesota & Eastern Railroad Corporation took over the IMRL's operations on July 31, 2002, renaming it the Iowa, Chicago & Eastern Railroad (IC&E). On October 30, 2008, Canadian Pacific acquired the IC&E and the railroad has operated since then under CP's control.

Over the years, this line has been broken up several different ways, both by subdivision and by full division. Towards the end of the Milwaukee Road, it was the Northern Division, with the Twenty-Fifth Subdivision to the east of Mason City. Today, this line runs between Marquette and Sheldon, Iowa, and is broken down into the Mason City Subdivision to the east of Mason City, all part of the U.S. East Region of Canadian Pacific.

106.6 NORA SPRINGS – Trains moving from the Iowa Northern to the Canadian Pacific use an interchange track in the northeast quadrant of the diamond at Nora Junction. A northbound train on the Iowa Northern can back around this connecting track and onto the tracks of Canadian Pacific in the Nora Springs area. Once the train is on the CP mainline, it is facing west and can head straight to Garner. Because of this, the Nora Springs station is listed here.

Nora Springs was founded on May 23, 1857, with the name Woodstock. With little growth, Edward P. Greeley offered to buy twenty acres of the town, build a store, and acquire and improve the existing mill if the town was renamed Elnora, after a woman in Vermont whom Greeley hoped to marry. After some debate, the name Nora Springs was agreed upon. With the town named after this prospective bride, Greeley returned to Vermont to propose marriage, but was rejected by Elnora. Greeley was furious and never returned to Nora Springs, selling off his properties. The town was finally incorporated on September 17, 1874.

The population of Nora Springs was 1369 in 2020. The community is the home of the annual Nora Springs Buffalo Days festival, scheduled for the last week of June. The festival includes a parade, entertainment, food vendors, a 5K run-walk, a softball tournament, a fireman's ball, and other events.

106.9 SHELL ROCK RIVER BRIDGE – The Shell Rock River is a tributary of the Cedar River flowing south from Albert Lea Lake in Freeborn County, Minnesota. The United States Board on Geographic Names settled on "Shell Rock River" as the stream's name in

1931. It has also been known by the spelling "Shell-rock River."

For many years, this was a 138-foot single span Warren through truss bridge, built by the Lassig Bridge & Iron Works of Chicago, Illinois. It has been replaced by a two-span plate girder bridge.

107.3 NORA JUNCTION – Located southwest of Nora Springs, Iowa, this is the junction between Canadian Pacific and Iowa Northern that is used to head west to the IANR Garner Subdivision. A map from 1875 showed an active area at what was known as Nora Junction. The map showed a second connection between the two railroads in the southwest quadrant, with several blocks of a platted community where Larson's Salvage now stands. The map also showed a joint depot in the southwest corner of the diamond, and a hotel across the Rock Island tracks. The community of Nora Junction featured a grain warehouse. IANR trains taking this route often have locomotives on each end of the train to allow the switch backs here and at Garner.

107.7 COUNTY LINE – **Floyd County** is to the east while **Cerro Gordo County** is to the west. **Floyd County** was established in January 1851 and officially organized as of August 1854. Where the name Floyd came from is unknown, but there are at least three explanations. The first, and probably the most widely-held belief is that the county was named for Sergeant Charles Floyd, a member of the famed Lewis and Clark Expedition, who died in 1804 during the trip and was buried just south of present-day Sioux City. His death and burial were the first ever recorded in Iowa.

A second explanation is that Floyd County was named in honor of William Floyd of Long Island, New York, one of the signers of the Declaration of Independence. A third explanation is that the county was named after former Virginia governor and Secretary of War, John Buchanan Floyd. This latter explanation caused some to try to rename the county after John Buchanan Floyd joined the Confederate Army as a general during the Civil War. That effort was aborted, though, after Senator John F. Duncombe of Fort Dodge assured people that the county was indeed named after Charles Floyd.

In 2020, the county's population was 15,627. Its county seat is Charles City.

Cerro Gordo County was in the early days of the state a part of Fayette County. The first white settlers came to the new county in 1851. As the population grew, a courthouse was established in Mason City in 1857. It was short-lived because in the summer of 1857, the county seat was moved to Livonia. A new courthouse was built there, and the county records and offices were soon located at this small town. This too was short-lived, because in April 1858, Mason City won back the county seat in an election.

The county is named after the location of a battle in the Mexican War. At Cerro Gordo, General Winfield Scott defeated General Santa Ana of the Mexican army on April 18, 1847. The battle was significant because it opened the way for the United States to take Mexico City. The Spanish translation of Cerro Gordo is "fat hill." Near the west side of Cerro Gordo County is the site of the airplane crash that killed Buddy Holly, Ritchie Valens, and J. P. "The Big Bopper" Richardson on February 3, 1959.

Cerro Gordo County is somewhat unique for northern Iowa as it has a large number of manufacturing plants, generally around Mason City. Because of this, the county has a higher population than most counties in the area, with 43,127 residents in the 2020 census.

112.8 PORTLAND – On June 7, 1855, Alonza S. Felt arrived in the area and began buying land. By 1856, he owned more than 1000 acres in the area. The McGregor & Missouri River Railway reached here in 1870, and a spur track was built within a few years. A post office opened at Portland in 1874. In 1878, Felt laid out a small town around the spur track, naming it Portland, the same as the local township and post office. Felt worked hard to make the village a success. He planted shade trees along the streets, and provided land for businesses such as a blacksmith shop, the Portland Cheese Factory (1879), and the second store building (1880). A flour mill was later built in the area. However, with Mason City so close, little actually developed at Portland.

Portland is at the bottom of a hill with uphill grades of 0.7-0.8% in each direction. To the south is the North Iowa Cooperative facility, served by a short industry siding and spur track. The population of the Village of Portland was 28 in 2020.

113.1 WINNEBAGO RIVER BRIDGE – The Winnebago River is a wandering river that is about 70 miles long. It starts north of Forest City, flows south and then turns east and passes through Mason City. Near here, the river turns to the southeast and flows into the Shell Rock River near Rockford, Iowa. The stream was once known as Lime Creek, but was declared to be the Winnebago River by the U.S. Board on Geographic Names in 1961. The river was named for the local Winnebago Indians.

The 124-foot-long bridge is a unique Pony truss bridge, a truss bridge without a connecting top. The bridge was built by F. B. Walker in August 1908. F. B. Walker held a number of railroad engineering positions over the years, including Resident Engineer for the Northern Pacific Railway and Great Northern Railway, as well as Chief Engineer for the Eastern Massachusetts Street Railway Company in Boston, Massachusetts.

114.0 DIVISION LINE – This was once a division line between different parts of the railroad. In 1962, for the Chicago, Milwaukee, St. Paul & Pacific Railroad, to the east was the Dubuque & Illinois Division while to the west was the Iowa, Minnesota & Dakota Division.

115.0 EAST SWITCH – This is the east switch to the Mason City complex. There are two sidings here, each approximately 0.75 miles long.

116.3 9TH STREET CROSSING – This crossing, located a block east of the South Carolina grade crossing, was once with the Minneapolis & St. Louis Railway, which operated from Manly south to Mason City, adjacent to the Rock Island route. The track north of here was abandoned in 1970, and then through town in 1988, after being acquired by the Chicago & North Western.

116.7 MASON CITY – Just west of 9th Street Crossing is the Mason City Yard and a junction with the Owatonna Subdivision, which heads to the northeast to Comus, Minnesota. Mason City Yard features a small locomotive shop, turntable, and about a dozen tracks. On the north side of the yard is the former Milwaukee Road station, built of brick and stone, used by the railroad for offices. Some recent reports have plans for the station to be torn down and new offices built.

This railroad station can be found at Mason City, Iowa. Located on South Pennsylvania Avenue, this former Chicago, Milwaukee, St. Paul & Pacific station has been used as a railroad office, but there has been some discussion about tearing the station down.

In 1909, there were a number of facilities along the railroad in this area. On the north side of the yard near its east end was the Mason City Transfer & Storage Company, with several Standard Oil warehouses immediately to the west. Further west was the railroad ice house and platform. There were a number of railroad buildings and offices around the depot location. Today, the depot is located just west of Pennsylvania Avenue, what was known as Rawlins in 1909. On the corner of Rawlins were two hotels – Stanton Hotel to the east and Collin's Hotel & Lunch Room to the west. Just east of the passenger station was a railroad office and storage facility, about the same size as the station. Just to the north of the office was the railroad's freight house at Kearney, now South Jersey Avenue. On the south side of the yard across from the station was a roundhouse and machine shop.

There are other stations that still stand in Mason City. The former Chicago Great Western station is located at 540 1st Street NW, alongside tracks currently operated by Union Pacific. A modern Minneapolis & St. Louis station, built in 1955 and still used by Union Pacific, is located at 436 3rd Street NE. The railroad's concrete block engine house built in 1948 is located several blocks to the north and is used for storage by a ready-mix concrete plant.

Plymouth Junction to Mason City
Canadian Pacific Owatonna Subdivison

The line between Plymouth Junction and Mason City was built in 1870 by the Mason City & Minnesota Railway Company. The Mason City & Minnesota (MC&M) was incorporated on July 18, 1870, to build a line toward Minnesota as an effort to work with the Iowa Central Rail Road to move coal from the Fort Dodge area. By the end of the year, the railroad had built 28 miles of track from Mason City, Iowa, to the Iowa/Minnesota state line. On January 9, 1871, the railroad was turned over to the Milwaukee & St. Paul, which became the Chicago, Milwaukee & St. Paul Railway (CM&StP) in 1874. The CM&StP declared bankruptcy in 1925 and reorganized as the Chicago, Milwaukee, St. Paul & Pacific Railroad in 1928.

In 1959, this route was the Third Subdivision of the Iowa, Minnesota and Dakota Division. As with many former Milwaukee Road lines, after the company's bankruptcy, the line was acquired by the Soo Line, a part of Canadian Pacific.

In 1997, the I&M Rail Link (IMRL) acquired this line from Canadian Pacific/Soo Line. After several years of economic problems, the Dakota, Minnesota & Eastern Railroad Corporation took over the IMRL's operations on July 31, 2002, renaming it the Iowa, Chicago & Eastern Railroad (IC&E). On October 30, 2008, Canadian Pacific acquired the IC&E and the railroad has operated since then under CP's control as the Owatonna Subdivision.

7.4 **PLYMOUTH JUNCTION** – "At Plymouth Junction, the normal position of the electrically locked gate at the CRI&P RR crossing is against movements on the CMStP&P RR. All trains on the CMStP&P RR must stop at the Stop sign regardless of the position of the gate and must not proceed beyond this sign nor may the gate be swung until any train or engine approaching on the CRI&P RR has either passed over the crossing or come to a stop." This is how the Milwaukee Road 1959 employee timetable described the control of the Plymouth Junction diamond, also known as CRI&P Crossing.

Today, the Canadian Pacific timetable shows this as an "IANR Crossing." There is an interchange track to the east of this diamond. For northbound Iowa Northern trains, they turn to the northeast to enter the Owatonna Subdivision of the Canadian Pacific, leading to the need to have trackage rights starting at Milepost 7.9. After the Iowa Northern train enters the CP, it is facing the wrong way to head to Mason City and on to Garner. This means that trains making this move typically have locomotives on each end.

0.0 **MASON CITY** – This is Milepost 116.7 on the Canadian Pacific main east-west line. Just west of 9th

Street Crossing is the Mason City Yard and a junction with the Mason City Subdivision, which heads to the east to Marquette, Iowa.

Mason City to Garner
Canadian Pacific Sheldon Subdivision

The track west of Mason City was built by the McGregor & Missouri River Railway in 1870 using available land grants. It was soon absorbed by its parent company, the Milwaukee & St. Paul, which became the Chicago, Milwaukee & St. Paul Railway (CM&StP) in 1874. The CM&StP declared bankruptcy in 1925 and reorganized as the Chicago, Milwaukee, St. Paul & Pacific Railroad in 1928.

After the failure of the Milwaukee Road, the line was acquired by the Soo Line, a part of Canadian Pacific. In 1997, the I&M Rail Link (IMRL) acquired this line from Canadian Pacific/Soo Line. After several years of economic problems, the Dakota, Minnesota & Eastern Railroad Corporation took over the IMRL's operations on July 31, 2002, renaming it the Iowa, Chicago & Eastern Railroad. On October 30, 2008, Canadian Pacific acquired the IC&E and the railroad has operated since then under CP's control.

Over the years, this line has been broken up several different ways, both by subdivision and by full division. Towards the end of the Milwaukee Road, it was the Twenty-Sixth Subdivision of the Northern Division. Today, this line runs between Marquette and Sheldon, Iowa, and is the Sheldon Subdivision to the west of Mason City, part of the U.S. East Region of Canadian Pacific.

116.7 MASON CITY – Heading west, the railroad passes along the south side of downtown, creating junctions with several other railroads.

Mason City started with the farm of John B. Long, who settled at the confluence of the Winnebago River and Calmus Creek in 1851. Long named his farm Masonic Grove, and soon partnered with several others to establish a community named Shibboleth on his property. By 1854, Long bought out his partners and renamed the town after his son Mason. The next year, the name was changed to Mason City. The town was incorporated on December 21, 1869. It later became the county seat of Cerro Gordo County. The population of Mason City was 27,338 in the 2020 census.

Mason City grew around the Winnebago River, giving it the nickname of River City. This became even more famous when Meredith Willson, who grew up in Mason City and played in the Mason City Symphonic Band as a high school student, wrote the musical *The Music Man*. Willson said that the musical was based upon life in Mason City and many of the people that he knew.

117.2 BEAR TRAP JUNCTION – This is the diamond with the Union Pacific Mason City Subdivision. There is a connecting track to the southeast, but it does not directly connect with the Mason Subdivision, but instead with the remains of a line to the southeast, now known as the Rockwell Industrial Lead.

117.8 IOWA TRACTION TRANSFER TRACK – To the south are the electrified tracks of the Iowa Traction Railway, founded in 1896 as the Mason City & Clear Lake Railway. The railroad became the Mason City & Clear Lake Railroad in 1950, the Mason City Division of the Iowa Terminal Railroad in 1961, the Iowa

Traction Railroad in 1987, and then Iowa Traction Railway in 2012.

This is the last electric freight railroad in Iowa. It is somewhat unique in that freight has always been the primary revenue source. Passenger service began on July 4, 1897, and ended on August 30, 1936.

Iowa Traction freight motor #50, built by Baldwin in 1920, serves a grain complex near Mason City.

119.8 CARTERSVILLE ELEVATOR – To the south are several tracks which serve this elevator, once the Allied Mills facility. Just west of the elevator is a track south to the Renewable Energy Group's biodiesel production facility, also served by the Iowa Traction Railway. The plant opened in 2007 and was acquired by Chevron Renewable Energy Group in June 2013. It has the capacity to manufacture approximately 30 million gallons of biodiesel each year. Today, Chevron Renewable Energy Group is one of the largest biodiesel producers by volume in the United States.

120.6 BEHR IRON & METAL – This is another spur to the south to serve a Mason City shipper. Behr Iron & Metal operated solely in the metal recycling industry in Illinois, Iowa and Wisconsin. This facility was one of three that also incorporated an automobile shredder. The Iowa Traction Railway serves the scrap yard from the south, the location of their shops and office.

During late 2016, Alter Trading Corporation and its Alter Metal Recycling company acquired the operating assets of Behr Iron & Metal. This included this Mason City facility, which helped to make Alter one of the largest recyclers of ferrous and non-ferrous metals in the country. The Mason City facility is home to one of the automobile shredders. This football field-length machine can shred one to two cars per minute.

Heading west, the railroad bridges over Willow Creek several times.

124.7 INTERSTATE 35 – The railroad passes under I-35, the ninth-longest of all Interstate Highways and the third-longest north-south Interstate Highway. It stretches 1568 miles from Laredo, Texas, to Duluth, Minnesota.

125.5 NORTH IOWA COOPERATIVE – This a sister facility to the cooperative elevator at Portland. The North Iowa Cooperative has five facilities, located at Clear Lake, Plymouth, Portland, Thornton, and United L.P. at Mason City.

126.2 CLEAR LAKE – Look for the siding to the south. Clear Lake is a growing lake community and suburb of Mason City. It had a population of 7,687 in the 2020 census. In 1851, Joseph Hewitt and James Dickirson arrived on Clear Lake and began building cabins and farms. 1855 saw a school built, a hotel open, and a sawmill open. The town grew quickly with 775 residents in 1870 when the railroad built through the area. The town of Clear Lake was incorporated on May 26, 1871, and was already a resort community due to the lake. A series of parks and attractions were built around the lake, with the Bayside Amusement Park opening in 1909, and closing in 1958. The North Iowa Band Festival started in 1932 and added to the attractions.

After a fire, the Tom Tom Ballroom was rebuilt as the Surf Ballroom in 1933. The new facility burned in 1947 and a modern Surf Ballroom opened up across the street the next year. The Surf Ballroom was regionally famous, and many major acts performed there. The ballroom became a part of an infamous event when a number of famous rock-and-roll performers sang there and then died leaving Clear Lake. After performing on February 2, 1959, Buddy Holly, Ritchie Valens, and J. P. "The Big Bopper" Richardson died when their Beechcraft Bonanza aircraft crashed soon after takeoff, killing everyone aboard. The incident later was eulogized in the song *American Pie* by Don McLean.

131.0 VENTURA – There are several tracks to the south to serve the Five Star Cooperative complex. Five Star was founded in 1916 with 19 locations throughout Northeast & North Central Iowa.

This location was first known as Thayer's Siding when the community was created on November 16, 1885. Some reports state that the name was supposed to be changed to Venture, but an error led it to be named Ventura. The town was officially incorporated on May 28, 1960.

131.9 COUNTY LINE – Look for the grade crossing with Apple Lane at the west end of Ventura. The county line is at the top of a low ridge through the area, the top of grades from both east and west on the railroad. **Cerro Gordo County** is to the east while **Hancock County** is to the west.

Cerro Gordo County was in the early days of the state a part of Fayette County. The first white settlers came to the new county in 1851. As the population grew, a courthouse was established in Mason City in 1857. It was short-lived because in the summer of 1857, the county seat was moved to Livonia. A new courthouse was built there, and the county records and offices were soon located at this small town. This too was short-lived, because in April 1858, Mason City won back the county seat in an election.

The county is named after the location of a battle in the Mexican War. At Cerro Gordo, General Winfield Scott defeated General Santa Ana of the Mexican army on April 18, 1847. The battle was significant because it opened the way for the United States to take Mexico City. The Spanish translation of Cerro Gordo is "fat hill." Near the west side of Cerro Gordo County is the site of the airplane crash that killed Buddy Holly, Ritchie Valens, and J. P. "The Big Bopper" Richardson on February 3, 1959.

Cerro Gordo County is somewhat unique for northern Iowa as it has a large number of manufacturing plants, generally around Mason City. Because of this, the county has a higher population than most counties in the area, with 43,127 residents in the 2020 census.

Hancock County was founded on January 15, 1851, and named after John Hancock, a signer of the *U.S. Declaration of Independence*. The county was officially organized on November 25, 1858. Garner is the county seat. The county is generally rural, with a population of 10,795 in 2020. This is less than 20 residents per square mile. The county lies at the headwaters of the Iowa, Boone, and Des Moines Rivers, and was considered neutral territory between the Sioux to the north and the Winnebagoes to the south. The first farm reportedly was planted in 1854. Heading west, the railroad is back again in rural farmland.

134.3 TANK SPUR – Milwaukee Road records show that this was a Monsanto facility. Today, it is the CF Industries Garner Terminal, located to the south of the mainline. This terminal supplies ammonia and urea ammonium nitrate (UAN), both used as fertilizers.

134.9 HILL SPUR – There are two facilities here, Koch Nitrogen and the Nutrien Garner Distribution Terminal. Both provide products to the local agricultural industry.

137.5 GARNER – This is the junction and diamond with the former Chicago, Rock Island & Pacific line that was later acquired by the Chicago & North Western, then Union Pacific. Today, it is operated by the Iowa Northern and is owned by the North Central Iowa Rail Corridor, LLC.

The town of Garner was platted in the summer of 1870 by John Maben and the McGregor & Missouri River Railway, later the Chicago, Milwaukee & St. Paul Railway. The plat was officially filed on August

23, 1870. A post office also opened in 1870. A grain warehouse opened the next year. Garner was named after Colonel W. W. Garner, a civil engineer on the Rock Island Railroad, and the town was incorporated in 1881. Garner was home to the Fred and August Duesenberg bicycle shop in the 1880s. These brothers later went on to build the Duesenberg auto famous for its racing ability. Today, Garner is the county seat of Hancock County. The population was 3065 in the 2020 census, a small increase from 2922 in the 2000 census.

Belmond to Forest City
Garner Subdivision

On September 12, 1870, the Iowa & Minnesota Railroad Company was incorporated "to construct, operate and maintain a railroad from the north line of Winnebago County, Iowa to or near Fort Dodge and thence in a southwesterly direction to the Missouri River at such point as the Board of Directors may hereafter establish." The plan was to build a railroad from Forest City to Belmond, Iowa, with stations at Miller, Hayfield Junction, Garner, Klemme, and Goodell. The railroad was sold on November 21, 1883, to the Cedar Rapids, Iowa Falls & Northwestern Railway Company (CRIF&NW), which had been founded on June 4, 1880.

The CRIF&NW was a holding and construction company created and controlled by the Burlington, Cedar Rapids & Northern Railway Company (BCR&N) "to locate, construct, maintain and operate a railway with all the necessary branches, warehouses, elevators and such other appendages as may be deemed necessary for the convenient use and profitable management of the same from the town of Holland, Grundy County, Iowa by way of Iowa Falls to some point in the State of Minnesota, yet to be determined." The railroad expanded the rail routes by building a branch from Belmond to Dows (15 miles) in 1884, and Forest City to Armstrong, Iowa (46 miles), by 1892.

The railroad built from Hayfield Junction to Hayfield, Iowa, by 1884, connecting with the Des Moines & Fort Dodge Railroad, which became the Minneapolis & St. Louis. For a time, trains ran over the Des Moines & Fort Dodge Railroad from Hayfield/Madison to Forest City, until the

Garner-Forest City line opened in 1895. Meanwhile, the railroad built to the northwest from Forest City to Armstrong, Iowa. The Burlington, Cedar Rapids & Northern purchased the Cedar Rapids, Garner & Northwestern on July 11, 1900, and the Cedar Rapids, Iowa Falls & Northwestern in 1902, consolidating all of the lines.

While the Rock Island has been abandoned between Belmond and Dows, the depot at Dows still remains.

By this time, the BCR&N was controlled by the Chicago, Rock Island & Pacific Railway Company (CRIP) through majority stock purchase (the majority purchase took place on July 15, 1885). The control of these companies by the CRIP was designed to move Minnesota and northern Iowa traffic to its mainline at West Liberty, and then over the CRIP mainline to Chicago. To further control the BCR&N, it was leased by the CRIP on June 1, 1902, and then fully acquired on June 15, 1903.

Passenger service on this line was never heavy, with little through service. In 1949, this line was served by several passenger trains, none of which were much more than local service. South of Garner, train #19-435 came up from Cedar Rapids in the early morning and returned in the afternoon as #436-20. North of Garner, mixed train #437 left at 9:25am, fifteen minutes after the arrival of #19-435.

Southbound, mixed train #438 passed Forest City at noon with a scheduled arrival in Garner at 12:50pm, seventy minutes before #436-20 departed back for Cedar Rapids. During the 1950s, the *Official Guide* showed that this line had "Mixed Service Only" operating "Subject to local operating conditions." By 1961, the line was shown to be "Freight Service Only."

Under the Rock Island, this line was a typical rural agricultural railroad. However, there was enough business that it was still listed as Subdivision 12b (Forest City Branch) of the Northern Division in 1974, and the Des Moines Division in 1979. On June 29, 1983, the Chicago & North Western (CNW) acquired the CRIP Minneapolis-Kansas City mainline as well as a number of branch lines, including the line to Forest City. In 1994, the line was shown as the Klemme Subdivision, covering Forest City (milepost 157.5) to Belmond (milepost 128.0). Almost the entire line at the time was limited to 10 miles per hour and grain trains were restricted to no more than 50 cars.

The line became the property of Union Pacific (UP) after they acquired the CNW in 1995. After the mid-1990s, UP changed the mileposts when it consolidated the line between Moorland, Iowa, and Forest City. The line, known as the Klemme Branch, then became known as the Fort Dodge Subdivision.

In 2010-2011, efforts took place to save the line as UP had started plans to abandon it. To quote the Surface Transportation Board filing, "North Central Iowa Rail Corridor, LLC (NCIRC), a noncarrier, has filed a verified notice of exemption under 49 CFR 1150.31 to acquire approximately 27.83 miles of rail line owned by Union Pacific Railroad Company (UP), referred to as the Forest City Line. The Forest City Line extends between milepost 48.12 at Belmond, Iowa, and milepost 79.95 at Forest City, Iowa, and includes 600 feet of connecting track at Garner, Iowa, in Hancock,

Winnebago, and Wright Counties, Iowa." The North Central Iowa Rail Corridor was created by Forest City and Garner grain elevators, farmers, and manufacturer Winnebago Industries. The reported price was $1.5 million.

In the May 27, 2011, *Federal Register*, the Surface Transportation Board published a notice that the Iowa Northern Railway had applied "to operate approximately 27.83 miles of rail line owned by Union Pacific Railroad Company (UP), referred to as the Forest City Line." Also, the IANR had applied for trackage rights over the "Dakota, Minnesota & Eastern Railroad Corporation d/b/a Canadian Pacific."

The trackage rights included approximately 78.2 miles of rail line between:

[1] Milepost 137.5 near Garner, Iowa, and Milepost 116.7 at the connection with CP's Mason City Subdivision, a distance of approximately 20.8 miles;

[2] Milepost 116.7 at the connection with CP's Mason City Subdivision and Milepost 107.3 near Nora Junction, Iowa, at the connection with IANR, a distance of approximately 30.2 miles between Garner and Nora Jct.; and

[3] Milepost 116.7 at the connection with CP's Mason City Subdivision and Milepost 7.9 on CP's Austin Subdivision near Plymouth Junction, Iowa, at the connection with IANR, a distance of approximately 27.2 miles between Garner and Plymouth Junction.

These rights allow the Iowa Northern Railway to serve the Forest City Line from multiple locations on their Cedar Falls to Manly mainline. On the Iowa Northern, the route is now known as the Garner Subdivision. In 2019, the line between Belmond and Klemme was busy making the railroad money by storing railroad cars. These cars were primarily covered hopper cars for moving sand, and coal hoppers.

The initial lease of the line was for ten years, and in 2021, the lease was extended for another three years, from September 30, 2021, until September 30, 2024. However, no filing was made with the Surface Transportation Board, and in late 2023, a filing was made for after-the-fact Board authorization for the transaction.

The south end of the Garner Subdivision is often full of stored freight cars, making money for the Iowa Northern Railway. These cars are parked at Goodell.

FOREST CITY DIVISION.

No. 81	Mls	*May* 14, 1893.	Mls	No. 82
†1 10 P.M.		lv..**Iowa Falls**.ar.		4 40 P.M.
3 30 "	0	..... **Dows**....	96	3 00 "
3 45 "	7	...... Rowen...	89	2 43 "
4 08 "	15	+ **Belmond**[33]	81	2 24 "
4 21 "	20	..... Goodell ...	76	2 09 "
4 34 "	27	... .Klemmes.	69	1 54 "
4 55 "	33	+..**Garner**[85]..	63	1 40 "
5 15 "	41	..**Hayfield**[88].	55	1 20 "
5 32 "	48	**Forest City**[82]½	48	1 00 P.M.
6 58 "	59	....Thompson....	37	12 32 NO'N
6 19 "	68	..Buffalo Center..	28	12 11 NO'N
6 37 "	76	...**Germania**...	20	11 54 A.M.
7 05 "	87	....Swea City ...	9	11 23 "
7 30 P.M.	96	ar.**Armstrong**.lv	0	†11 00 A.M.

Schedule for the Forest City Division of the Burlington, Cedar Rapids & Northern Railway, from *Travelers' Official Guide of the Railway and Steam Navigation Lines in the United States and Canada*, June 1893, page 541.

Footage Capacity					
Sidings	Other Tracks	Station Numbers	↓ WEST STATIONS EAST ↑		M.P. from Cedar Rapids
......	3600	55090	DOWS ....RWYd TO		113.2
			6.4		
......	......	......	C&NW Crossing ....UX		119.6
			0.3		
......	750	55007	ROWAN		119.9
			7.9		
......	......	......	C&NW Crossing ....UX		127.8
			0.2		
......	2400	55015	BELMOND		128.0
			0.8		
......	......	......	C&NW Crossing ....UX		128.8
			4.7		
......	750	55020	GOODELL		133.5
			5.8		
......	7800	55026	KLEMME		139.3
			6.5		
......	2750	55033	GARNER ....BTO(N)		145.8
			0.3		
......	......	......	CMStP&P Crossing ....UX		146.1
			2.0		
......	......	55035	HAYFIELD JCT		148.1
			3.6		
......	E500	55039	MILLER		151.7
			5.8		
......	9000	55045	FOREST CITY		157.5
			10.6		
......	1700	55055	THOMPSON		168.1
			9.0		
......	2400	55064	BUFFALO CENTER		177.1
			63.9		

BRANCH LINE   SUBDIV 12B   DES MOINES DIV

Schedule for Subdivision 12B, Des Moines Division, from the Rock
Island's *Timetable No. 1,* March 18, 1979, page 41.

Route Guide
Iowa Northern Railway – Belmond to Forest City

46.7 BELMOND – Belmond was former CRIP milepost 128.0, and the Iowa Northern Garner Subdivision actually starts about 1½ miles north of here. The track from here northward to the former crossing of the Rock Island and Chicago Great Western has been abandoned and removed.

Welcome to Belmond, Iowa, the south end of the Iowa Northern's Garner Subdivision.

In 1912, the Rock Island was essentially the eastern limits of Belmond, but today, the town goes several blocks further east, including several public schools. The former Rock Island route through Belmond is now mostly a wide grassy strip and the Franklin Grove Heritage Trail. The Franklin Grove Trail is 3.4 miles long and starts just south of the former diamond north of town, heads south through the intersection of Belmond Road and Taylor Avenue southeast of town, and on to Luicks Creek.

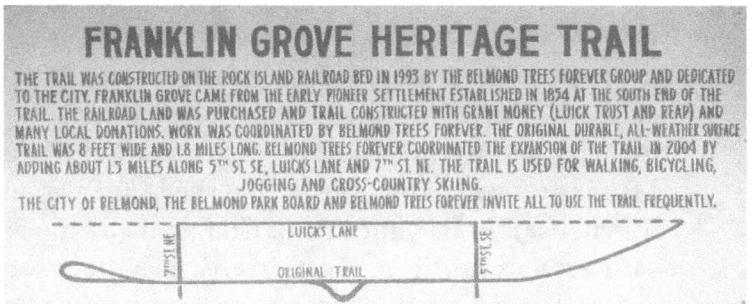

This sign marks the Franklin Grove Heritage Trail, which uses the abandoned Rock Island railroad grade through Belmond, Iowa.

In 1900, the Rock Island was lined with a number of industries through Belmond. The BCR&N depot was just north of Main Street, and south of Spruce. It was located east of the mainline. The use of the names Spruce and Main Streets can be confusing because during the late 1910s, the city renamed its streets, removing the many names and numbering them instead. Numbered Streets were used for east-west roads, while Avenues were used for north-south roads. Additionally, Spruce was renamed Main Street. This was because the Main Street on the east side of the Iowa River was one block south of Main Street on the west side of the Iowa River. With a bridge across the river on West Main, it made sense to rename the entire street Main Street.

The two-story wooden BCR&N depot had a long platform trackside, as well as a windmill-powered well at the north end of the depot. A 100,000-gallon water tank stood on a 14-foot trestle to the north with two tool houses further north about where the south switch of the siding to the west was located. East of the depot was a long house track serving (south to north) William Finch (south of 1900s Main Street with corn cribs, a coal shed, and a grain warehouse); E. D. Mineah and Company (a lumber yard located north of Main Street); J. N. Johnson & Co. (located north of Spruce and consisting of a 20,000-bushel grain elevator and a coal shed); and a stock yard with hog pen.

By 1921, there had been some changes. Located both north and south of the 1921 Main Street was the lumber and coal operation of Bock Lumber Company. The Rock Island's depot had moved according to the Sanborn Map Company, as it was now north of Main Street (once Spruce Street). To the north of 2nd Street, formerly Washington, was the 7000-bushel Farmers' Cooperative Elevator Company. The stockyards still remained further north, and the new United Manufacturing Company, makers of concrete mixers, was located north of where 3rd Street would be.

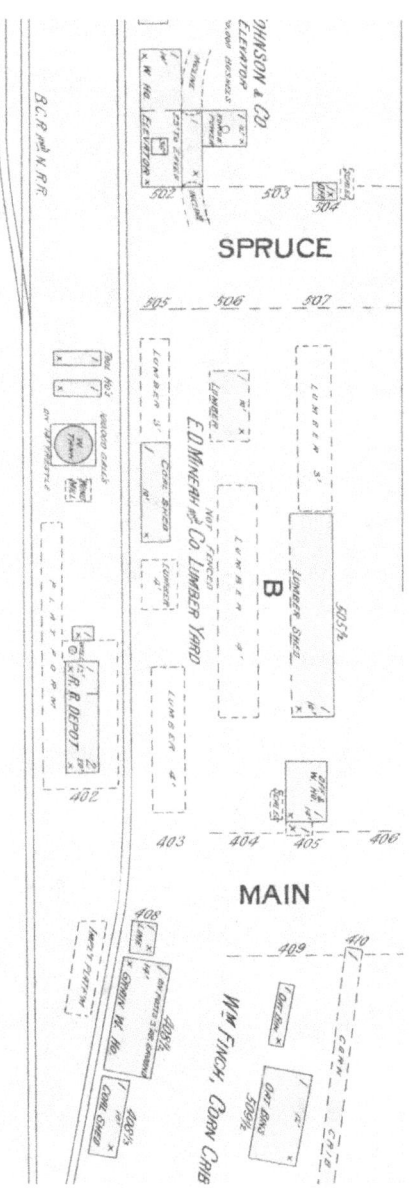

This Sanborn map of Belmond, Iowa, from 1900 shows how busy the area around the Burlington, Cedar Rapids & Northern depot was at that time. *Sanborn Fire Insurance Map from Belmond, Wright County, Iowa.* Sanborn Map Company, October 1900. Map. Retrieved from the Library of Congress, https://www.loc.gov/item/sanborn02578_002/.

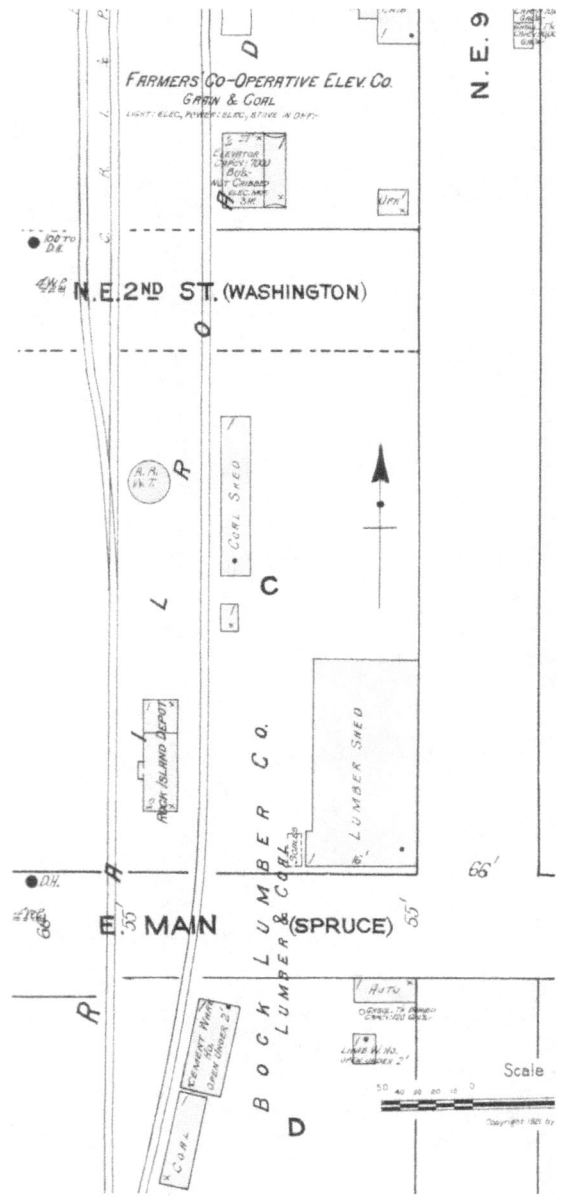

This Sanborn map from 1921 shows the changes around the Rock Island depot at Belmond, Iowa. *Sanborn Fire Insurance Map from Belmond, Wright County, Iowa.* Sanborn Map Company, August 1921. Map. Retrieved from the Library of Congress, https://www.loc.gov/item/sanborn02578_004/.

In the May 1921 issue of the *Rock Island Magazine*, there was an article about Belmond. At the time, the three railroads at Belmond had a combined daily service of sixteen passenger trains. The article stated that in addition to the new sugar beet industry, Belmond had a large brick, tile and cement plant, a modern grain elevator, and several flour mills. The new sugar mill had its own article as the movement of sugar beets and sugar was new to the Rock Island. The railroad was gaining new business from the mill, as well as the twenty-two thousand acres of beets that had been grown along the Rock Island in Northern Iowa the previous year. According to the Rock Island, the new mill was located south of Belmond and could slice 600 tons of beets a day, producing 1500 100-pound sacks of granulated sugar. The plant had twenty-one loaders to receive beets and to move them on to the Valley Sugar Company mill. The plant closed by World War II, and in early 1945, it reopened as a General Mills soybean processing plant with a capacity of 1,500,000 bushels. Belmond remained an active station on the Rock Island for several more decades, and the wooden depot was used into the 1960s. In 1974, the timetable showed that there were 2400 feet of side tracks here.

Chicago Great Western Railroad

On the north side of Belmond, the Rock Island and the Chicago Great Western once had a diamond and interchange track, allowing the railroads to cross each other and to swap loads of freight. With the Rock Island route south of here gone, Union Pacific and Iowa Northern use the former Chicago Great Western route into Belmond.

The Mason City & Fort Dodge Railway Company was incorporated on June 10, 1881, "to construct, acquire, and operate a railroad from a connection with the Chicago Great Western Railway Company's tracks at Hayfield, Minn., southwesterly through the cities of Mason City and Fort Dodge, Iowa, to Omaha, Nebr., and Sioux City, Iowa, with a line extending westerly from Oelwein, Iowa, to Clarion, Iowa, and branches from Fort Dodge to Lehigh, Iowa, and elsewhere as determined." In 1886, the railroad built 72.6 miles of track between Mason City and Fort Dodge, passing through Belmond. This construction allowed coal mined around Fort Dodge to reach markets to the north.

In 1900, the railroad had a number of facilities and customers on the west side of the Iowa River at the West Main Street grade crossing. From north to south was the Belmond Iowa Creamery Company (east of the tracks); C. L. Furuseth & Company (a 25,000-bushel grain elevator to the west just north of Main); Richardson & Kaufman (a 12,000-bushel grain warehouse south of Main Street and on the west side of the tracks); E. D. Mineah & Company (a lumber yard south of Main Street and to the east); and the depot a short distance further south.

On November 1, 1901, the Mason City & Fort Dodge was leased by the Chicago Great Western Railway Company (CGW). Several new incorporations of the Mason City & Fort Dodge took place in 1902 and 1905, and some lines were swapped between the two railroads to streamline operations. The two companies also owned each others' stock for some time. In 1921, the coal sheds of Belmond Lumber Company stood to the north of West Main Street on the east side of the tracks, while south of Main stood the Moore Grain Company on the west side of the tracks. This facility included a 12,000-bushel elevator and a 10,000-bushel warehouse. This is where the old elevator complex stands today.

The former CGW depot was on the west side of the Iowa River near Main Street. This line once came in from Mason City, but the route from here to Thornton was abandoned by Union Pacific in 2000. The route to the southwest toward Fort Dodge is still in place as UP's Fort Dodge Subdivision.

Just south of town on this line is the large MaxYield Cooperative grain facility. At this location was once the Iowa Valley Sugar Company, which produced granulated beet sugar and by-products. What was known as the Belmond Sugar Beet Factory was erected by the Iowa Valley Sugar Company in 1920. It had the capacity to process 700 tons of beets per day. Starting in 1928, the mill was owned by the American Beet Sugar Company, but a large fire in a warehouse containing 167,000 one-hundred-pound sacks of sugar set the firm back. The fire, which burned on March 20, 1929, brought fire departments from eight communities to try to save the processing plant, which did survive.

The next few years saw a slowing of production, and American Beet Sugar became the American Crystal Sugar Company in 1934. The plant closed in 1936 after several years of poor crops, and the plant was sold to General Mills in 1943, and to Central Soya in 1983, which demolished much of the facility that year.

The large MaxYield Cooperative grain facility towers over Belmond, Iowa.

Minneapolis & St. Louis Railroad

The third railroad in Belmond was the Iowa Central & Northwestern, with the original line to Belmond being built in 1881 from Hampton, Iowa. In 1882, the Central Iowa absorbed several railroads created for new construction, and became the owner of the track to Belmond. The Central Iowa Railway Company went into foreclosure and was reorganized as the Iowa Railway Company in 1888, but then was sold to the Iowa Central Railway Company on May 16, 1889.

The new organization soon led to plans for more railroads across Iowa. The *Mount Vernon Hawk-Eye* of November 11, 1898, reported that "another extension of the Iowa Central will be built from Belmond, the present termination of a branch, to Algona and possibly later will be run into the Dakotas." The

Iowa Central & Western Railroad was created for the project.

The Iowa Central was the east-west railroad in town, forming a large triangle around downtown Belmond. East of Race Street (today's 2nd Avenue), the railroad ran south of Rail Road Street. This area was also full of industry. West to east, these included the McGuire Elevator (a capacity of 13,000 bushels on the south side of the tracks); Richardson & Kaufman (a 20,000-bushel elevator, also to the south); the railroad depot to the north across from R&K and just west of Market Street (today's 4th Avenue); a 52,000-gallon water tower to the north; and H. J. Klemme Lumber Company (a lumber yard on the south side of the tracks).

On January 1, 1912, the Iowa Central was sold to The Minneapolis & St. Louis Railroad Company (M&StL). By 1921, there had been a few changes as the Farmers Cooperative Elevator Company had built in 1918 a 9-bin concrete 40,000-bushel elevator west of 5th Avenue on the south side of the M&StL. The H. J. Klemme Lumber Company was still in existance. The M&StL crossed the Rock Island several blocks south of the CRIP station.

The former M&StL east to Alexander was abandoned by the Chicago & North Western in 1981. The former CGW route to the southwest, and the M&StL to the northwest, both still remain and are operated by Union Pacific. All of these lines connect together at the former diamond, near the large MaxYield cooperative grain elevator on the southwest side of town.

City of Belmond

Belmond, originally located on the west side of the Iowa River, was founded on October 20, 1856. It was platted by Archer Dumond, James M. Elder and William E. Rogers, but there was no agreement about a name. Reportedly, Archer Dumond wanted to call it Crown Point after his earlier Indiana home, but others wanted to name it Dumond to honor the head of the group. However, there was already a Dumont, Iowa, and a new name was needed. Legend says that the new community was named for both Archer and his daughter, the first girl born in town. She was described as the "belle" of the community, thus Belmond.

A post office opened in 1856. On October 21, 1881, Belmond became an incorporated town by a vote of 51 to 47. By 1900, the population was approximately 1200, with 1800 by 1921. The population was 2463 in 2020, near its historical peak of 2560 in the year 2000. According to several sources, Belmond, Iowa, is the only town in the United States using that name.

The East Branch and the West Branch of the Iowa River merge just north of town. Belmond seems to be a center of natural disasters. On October 14, 1966, an F5 tornado ripped apart the community, destroying or damaging about 600 homes and 75 businesses. Six people were killed and large swaths of the town were left in ruins. Belmond was hit again during the June 2008 Midwest floods, with many parts of town under water. On June 12, 2013, an F3 tornado passed through the northern parts of town destroying several businesses and homes.

Belmond is still an agricultural town. There are good retail centers downtown and along U.S. Highway 69 on the west side of town. The Belmond-Kemme school systems has its facilities on the northeast side of town. Syngenta Seeds has a facility on the west side of town, but isn't served by the railroads. South of town is the large MaxYield Cooperative's dry fertilizer and grain facilities, located on the tracks of Union Pacific.

47.5   C&NW CROSSING – This was former CRIP milepost 128.8, and in 1974, the crossing was protected by stop signs. The CRIP once crossed the former Chicago Great Western line that ran between Mason City and Fort Dodge. This line and others were originally surveyed and graded by the Iowa Pacific. However, no track was built until the Mason City & Fort Dodge (MC&FD) constructed a line between the two towns in 1886. The MC&FD was leased to the Chicago Great Western in 1901. The route was extended on each end until it became a through route between the Twin Cities in Minnesota to Council Bluffs in Iowa. The line eventually became part of the Chicago & North Western,

Early maps show that there was an interchange track in the southeast corner of the diamond, and the Franklin Grove Heritage Trail's north end is in this location. The CGW line to the northeast was abandoned by Union Pacific in 2000, and the Forest City line became an extension of the line up from Fort Dodge. This explains the tight curve as the railroad today changes from heading northeast to heading to the north and then to the northwest.

48.1 EAST FORK IOWA RIVER BRIDGE – Just north of 130th Street (Milepost 47.9), the rail line crosses the East Fork Iowa River. The Iowa River is a 325-mile-long tributary of the Mississippi River. It rises in two branches, the West Branch and East Branch, both of which have their headwaters in Hancock County. The branches join together at Belmond, just a short distance downstream from here, to create the Iowa River. This bridge is 304 feet long and consists of six deck plate girder spans.

48.2 PROPERTY LINE – The property line (Milepost 48.12) between Union Pacific (to the south) and Iowa Northern Railway (to the north) is at the north end of the East Fork Iowa River bridge. Heading north, the railroad follows U.S. Highway 69 and climbs grades as much as 1.0% as it generally follows the river.

51.0 COUNTY LINE – The railroad crosses the county line at 100th Street and curves to the east to pass around Goodell. **Wright County** is to the south while **Hancock County** is to the north.

According to the county website, **Wright County** was organized in 1855. However, several other dates are provided by other sources. It is not clear where the name Wright came from. Some sources claim that the county was named for Andrew Wright, an early settler who operated several businesses and worked as a lawyer. Other sources claim that settlers named it for the governor of the state they came from. The most likely sources are Silas Wright, Governor of New York, and Joseph Wright, Governor of Indiana. The county seat is Clarion, and the population in 2020 was 12,943.

Hancock County was founded on January 15, 1851, and named after John Hancock, a signer of the *U.S. Declaration of Independence*. The county was officially organized on November 25, 1858. Garner is the county seat. The county is generally rural, with a population of 10,795 in 2020. This is less than 20 residents per square mile. The county lies at the headwaters of the Iowa, Boone, and Des Moines Rivers, and was considered neutral territory between the Sioux to the north and the Winnebagoes to the south. The first farm reportedly was planted in 1854.

52.2   GOODELL – Goodell was at former CRIP Milepost 128.8. In 1875, the grade for the Chicago, Iowa & Dakota Railway (locally known as the "Slippery Elm Railroad") was built through this area. While the line was built from Eldora Junction to Alden, all in Iowa, expansion ended when the contractor absconded with the company's funds and this part of the railroad was never completed. In 1884, the Iowa & Minnesota Railroad Company was built close to the original route. When the railroad missed the existing community of Amsterdam, a new community was created here. Eventually, Amsterdam shut down when the last store closed in 1888.

Goodell ("Little Town, Friendly People") was founded on December 16, 1884, when the depot was built along the railroad. It was first named Cashman for the man who built the grain elevator along the line, but the name soon changed to Goodell, after John Henry Goodell, one of the financial backers of the railroad. The Upper Grove post office moved here from nearby Amsterdam and changed its name to Goodell on October 28, 1885. The town was finally incorporated on February 3, 1893. By 1897, there were 34 businesses at Goodell, and its population peaked at 300 by 1914.

Goodell started as several blocks north and south of Broadway. On the north side of town was White's Addition, while Farnan's First and Second Additions were to the south. Later, Cline's Addition was platted east of the tracks. Today, Goodell is again about a dozen blocks of loosely settled lots north and south of Broadway. The population was 140 in the 2020 census.

This former elevator scale house stands next to the tracks at Goodell, Iowa.

Located at Third and Broadway is a brick building that looks like a train depot, but it faces the wrong way. It is in fact a scale house and office for what was once the local elevator. Note all of the model train signs in its windows. At one time Goodell had a two-story station, very similar to those built across Iowa on BCR&N lines. It was located on the west side of the mainline just north of Broadway, with a siding around the west side of the station. West of the siding was a lumber yard, with a grain elevator and then stock yards further to the north. All of this is now gone and the Iowa Northern has no side tracks at Goodell, although there were 750 feet of side tracks here in 1974.

Heading north, the railroad passes through miles of open farmland. This part of Iowa has been called "knobby" due to the number of small knolls and hillocks, basically sudden but small hills. Part of this is the Lau Wildlife Area, a public hunting area which the railroad passes north of 150th Street (Milepost 56.2).

57.2 EAST FORK IOWA RIVER BRIDGE – The railroad again crosses the East Fork of the Iowa River, here using a series of seven 35-foot deck plate girder spans.

58.0 KLEMME – This was former CRIP Milepost 139.3, and there were 7800 feet of side tracks here in 1974. Klemme ("Little But Lively") was surveyed and platted in 1889, with the documents filed on October 18, 1889. The town was incorporated on February 9, 1899. It was named for Harmon Johanas Klemme, the local property owner where the town was built. Klemme had worked with officials of the railroad to create the depot and town. The Klemme home is now the Klemme Homestead Museum at 112 South Second Street, two blocks to the east of the tracks.

Business soon developed and during November 1889, Henry Lau opened a grain buying and shipping station, as well as a lumber and coal business. More than 100 carloads of grain were shipped out that first year. A co-operative creamery was organized the next year, and the one-story wooden railroad station opened during December 1890.

An 1896 map showed that the depot was on the west side of the tracks just north of Main Street. There was a siding to the east, and a shorter one on the west side of the mainline, located just north of the depot. The track to the east served an elevator south of Main Street, a lumber yard opposite the station, and a grain elevator further north. There were stockyards north of the depot. Where this western track once was is today Railroad Street.

The Rock Island depot was once north of Main Street, where Railroad Street is now located.

Klemme still has a station sign, although all of the industry tracks have been retired.

Klemme has been the home of a number of industries. These include the Klemme Creamery, Koerner Dairy, and Schmidt Livestock Yards. There have been a number of grain elevators here, including Walter Bloom Elevator (1890s), Federal North Iowa Grain Company (early 1900s), and Klemme Cooperative Grain Company.

Today, there is the Five Star Cooperative, founded in 1916 with 19 locations throughout Northeast & North Central Iowa. Five Star Cooperative is a farmer-owned agricultural cooperative, based out of New Hampton, Iowa. It provides products and services in agronomy, energy, feed, grain, and even a hardware store. This is the Klemme Feedmill facility. MaxYield also has a facility here, greatly expanded over the past decade. The firm started when the West Bend Elevator Company (WBEC) was incorporated on May 29, 1915. In 2005, MaxYield Cooperative reached an agreement with AGP Grain Marketing that combined the operation of the Britt, Belmond, Garner, Klemme, and Meservey facilities. On August 1, 2021, MaxYield Cooperative merged with

Fort Dodge-based NEW Cooperative. Currently, no side tracks serve either elevator.

The population of Klemme was 441 during the 2020 census. The Klemme post office, opened in 1889, still exists. At the south edge of town is the Slippery Elm Golf Course.

The Five Star Cooperative has a feedmill elevator at Klemme, one of a number of agri businesses that have been here over the past century.

64.4 GARNER – The town of Garner was platted in the summer of 1870 by John Maben in conjunction with the McGregor & Missouri River Railway. The plat was officially filed on August 23, 1870. A post office also opened in 1870, and a grain warehouse opened the next year. Garner was named after Colonel W. W. Garner, a civil engineer on the Rock Island Railroad, and the town was incorporated in 1881. Garner was home to the Fred and August Duesenberg bicycle shop in the 1880s. These brothers later went on to build the Duesenberg automobile famous for its racing ability.

Although Garner already had a railroad with the Chicago, Milwaukee & St. Paul Railway, many of the leading citizens felt that a second railroad was needed to win the fight to be the county seat of Hancock County. Because of this, the line now operated by the Iowa Northern was encouraged to build through the town. Apparently, the plan was successful as today Garner is the county seat of Hancock County. The population was 3065 in the 2020 census, a small increase from 2922 in the 2000 census.

In an 1896 map, there is the "Hancock County Driving Park and Live Stock Association Grounds." It was located east of the Rock Island south of 12th Street. Part of this area is now a housing subdivision. A September 1900 Sanborn-Perris Map Company document showed that the Rock Island was very busy, centered around the 5th Avenue grade crossing. Just to the south and on the west side of the tracks was Reed, Harris & Company, a collection of warehouses, corn cribs and a grain elevator. Further south were stock yards. These were served by a siding west of the mainline. Just east of the mainline here was a large coal hopper with a raised trestle to feed it. Then there was a three-track yard further east.

Just north of the 5th Avenue grade crossing was the BCR&N "freight & passenger depot," located on the west side of the mainline. This was former CRIP milepost 145.8. Just north of the depot was a water tower and a windmill powering the water well. On the western siding were several coal sheds and the A. Schneider & Company 8000-bushel grain elevator. About three blocks further north, the Iowa Northern crosses at grade Canadian Pacific, once the Chicago, Milwaukee & St. Paul Railway.

Garner remained as the primary station along the Forest Branch even into the 1970s. As business on many of the Rock Island lines in Iowa decreased, many of the local trains that served the various lines were consolidated. During the 1960s and early 1970s, a local out of Iowa Falls would attempt to serve the industries in this area. A Garner Local, later simply called the Garner Switch Job, was based here to handle the Titonka and Lakota Branches. During the early 1970s, most of this work focused on Forest City where Winnebago received large volumes of truck frames used in manufacturing their motorhomes.

In 1974, there were 2750 feet of side tracks. The station housed general order boards and books. It was also a train order station, but had no train order signal. Thus, all trains on the branch stopped at Garner for train orders and instructions.

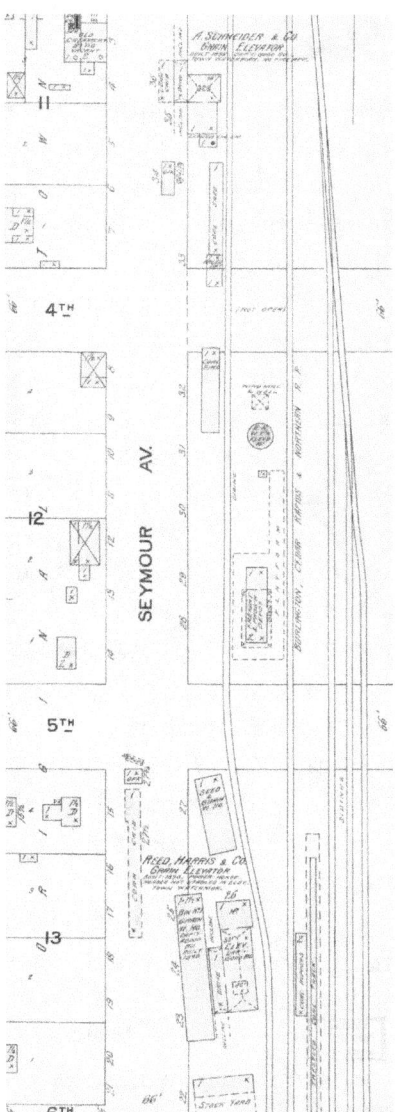

This Sanborn map from 1900 shows the Burlington, Cedar Rapids & Northern freight and passenger depot on the northeast corner of Seymour Avenue and Fifth. To its north was a railroad water tank, filled by a well powered by a windmill. *Sanborn Fire Insurance Map from Garner, Hancock County, Iowa.* Sanborn Map Company, September 1900. Map. Retrieved from the Library of Congress, https://www.loc.gov/item/sanborn02665_001/.

Today's Grain Elevators

Coming into Garner from the south, the railroad passes the Concord Cemetery and then several grain elevators. At Garner, the Iowa Northern has tracks into several parts of a grain elevator complex operated by MaxYield south of the diamond. The railroad also once served a small fertilizer facility to the north.

The elevators to the west tower over much of Garner, and are part of a series of changes that have been taking place in the grain-growing parts of the United States. The southernmost elevator still has the faint lettering for the Farmers Co-op Society. This organization had an elevator, creamery, and a lumber yard by 1913. By the late 1970s, the organization was shown to be the Farmers Coop Elevator Society in various government reports. This is not the only one of their elevators left in Garner. There is a red wooden Farmers Co-op Society elevator downtown at the State Street grade crossing of Canadian Pacific. This elevator was restored in 2009 but is used for other purposes.

Many of the elevator buildings along the Iowa Northern are now marked with signs for MaxYield Cooperative, a member-owned cooperative founded in 1915. The cooperative had 25 locations in Iowa and served its members with seed, agronomy, precision ag, data/information management, grain, energy, and feed. The Garner feed mill serves area small to mid-sized livestock operations.

Over the past decade, many of the smaller cooperatives have merged to gain volumes that give them more control over selling grains and buying seed and fertilizer. MaxYield was no exception as on August 1, 2021, the cooperative merged with the NEW Cooperative, headquartered in Fort Dodge, Iowa. The NEW Cooperative was formed in 1973 from two farmers' cooperatives in Northeast Webster County (NEW). This cooperative grew quickly with additional mergers and by acquiring other existing operations. The cooperative had almost 40 locations serving 5500 member-owners, and provided grain services, feed manufacturing, crop inputs and energy products. Even after the merger between NEW and MaxYield, the cooperative continued to expand. It bought several more elevators and then merged with the United Farmers Cooperative in 2023, expanding into Southern Iowa with twenty more locations.

Garner is a typical Iowa city where the grain elevators tower over the community. This one once belonged to the Garner Farmers Co-op Society.

64.7 **CPRS CROSSING** – Located at old CRIP milepost 146.1, this is the former McGregor & Missouri River Railway, built in the 1870s using available land grants. The McGregor & Missouri River Railway Company started as the McGregor & Sioux City Railway Company on January 23, 1868. It built a railroad from Calmar to Nora Springs, Iowa. This part of the railroad was conveyed to the Milwaukee & St. Paul Railway Company on May 1, 1869, and the land grants and construction rights became the McGregor & Missouri River Railway Company, which built on west through Garner to Algona, Iowa. On February 1, 1870, this property was also conveyed to the Milwaukee & St. Paul Railway. This became the Chicago, Milwaukee & St. Paul Railway Company on February 11, 1874.

For years, the Rock Island knew this location as CMStP&P Crossing. The Milwaukee depot was near Bush Avenue, and that railroad also had stock yards, a grain elevator (Spencer Grain Company), and a lumber yard (Woodford, Wheeler & Tompkins) in the area. On January 1, 1986, the Milwaukee Road was merged into the Soo Line Railroad, a subsidiary of Canadian Pacific Railway (CP). In 1997, the I&M Rail Link acquired this line from CP/Soo Line. After several years of economic problems, the Iowa, Chicago & Eastern Railroad took over the IMRL's operations on July 31, 2002. On October 30, 2008, Canadian Pacific acquired the IC&E and the railroad between Marquette and Sheldon, Iowa, has operated since then under CP's control. As of April 14, 2023, Canadian Pacific (CP) and Kansas City Southern (KCS) merged to create the only single-line railway connecting Canada, the U.S. and Mexico. The newly merged railroad uses the name Canadian Pacific Kansas City Limited (CPKC).

To the west and just south of the Canadian Pacific State Street grade crossing is the restored Farmers Co-op Society grain elevator. This wooden structure is today used for community meetings and is a great local feature.

A new interchange track was built in the southeast quadrant to allow Iowa Northern to reach this line. The crossing is still protected with a gate, lined against the Iowa Northern as it was historically for the Rock Island.

The CPRS Crossing at Garner is protected by a gate, lined against the Garner Subdivision of the Iowa Northern.

66.7 HAYFIELD JUNCTION – In this area, the railroad makes a smooth arc around the west end of a low ridge. By 1884, the Cedar Rapids, Iowa Falls & Northwestern Railway Company, a holding and construction company created and controlled by the Burlington, Cedar Rapids & Northern Railway Company, had built a line from here to the northwest to Hayfield, Iowa, a distance of about 8 miles. This route became the mainline of the railroad, as at Hayfield trains got on the line that became the Minneapolis & St. Louis to head north to Forest City, Iowa. This practice ended when the Rock Island built its own line to Forest City in 1895.

In 1898, the Cedar Rapids, Garner & Northwestern Railway Company was organized and extended the line westward another 18 miles to Titonka, Iowa. It soon fell under control of the Burlington, Cedar Rapids & Northern, and was assigned the route from Garner to Hayfield Junction and then to Titonka until the company was fully absorbed. The line was abandoned in 1980 with the end of the CRIP. This was CRIP Milepost 148.1.

70.3   MILLER – Miller was established on the property of W. L. Gordon, a surveyor, and E. C. Miller, a major property owner in the area. The community was named for Miller when the plat was filed on October 21, 1895. The town never grew much larger than 150 residents, but it was big enough for the Bank of Miller to be established in 1899.

In 1914, maps show Miller to be a collection of less than a dozen blocks to the east of the tracks. In 2019, Miller was a collection of less than a dozen houses surrounding Faith Lutheran Church along 290th Street. There are the remains of a grain elevator to the west of the tracks. In the 2010 census, the population was 60, and it was 50 in the 2020 census.

Miller was located at CRIP Milepost 151.7. In 1974, there was a 500-foot spur track. No side tracks exist here today. Heading north, the railroad experiences few grades and the line is generally straight until it reaches Forest City. The views continue to be of open farmland.

Miller still features a small grain elevator complex.

74.0 **DRAINAGE CANALS** – The railroad crosses several drainage canals between 320th Street (Milepost 73.7) and 325th Street (Milepost 74.2), with grades of 1% down to them from both directions. The canals drain the fields to the west, and the water flows into the Winnebago River to the east. This area has historically been used by several gravel pits. To the east is the Forest City Municipal Airport.

75.0 **HERITAGE PARK OF NORTH IOWA** – To the east is the Heritage Park of North Iowa, a 91-acre site with the goal of preserving the heritage of the area, to educate and to entertain, and to help the region's economy through tourism. The park hosts regular events, many based around the historic buildings that have been moved to the location. The park is new, being created in 2001 when the Winnebago Historical Society bought a 91-acre farm from Winnebago Industries.

Since the purchase, more than 40 buildings have been moved to the park. These include the Madison Schoolhouse which serves as the park's Railroad Museum, the Antique Transportation Museum with 10,000 square feet of antique vehicles, the Tractor Museum with 37,500 square feet of tractors, and the Steam Engine and Threshing Museum with approximately 30 steam engines and 40 threshing machines. The park also features one-half mile of track which is used by a gas-powered hydraulic drive locomotive capable of hauling 40 people.

Just south of this location, the Iowa Northern crosses U.S. Highway 69. This is a Minnesota to Texas cross-country route that is 1136 miles long. The north end of the highway is Albert Lea, Minnesota, while the south end is Port Arthur, Texas.

The Heritage Park of North Iowa features this motorcar shed with a Rock Island sign.

75.1 **FOREST CITY** – This is the official milepost for Forest City. The reason is that this is the switch that connects the two lines that serve Forest City industry. The former Rock Island tracks continue a short distance to the northwest. Meanwhile, this is a connection to a short piece of Minneapolis & St. Louis (M&StL) track that serves an agricultural facility to the northeast. The old Minneapolis & St. Louis station still stands near the cooperative's elevator. A description of what remains of both lines are included here.

Former Rock Island Line

75.1 **FOREST CITY** – This is the official milepost for Forest City, and is the junction switch connecting the Rock Island tracks with the Minneapolis & St. Louis tracks.

75.2 **C&NW/MSTL OVERPASS** – Look for the through plate girder span, set on timber piers with timber spans on each end. At one time, the Minneapolis & St. Louis passed under the CRIP at this location. This line was built by two railroads, the Minnesota & Iowa Southern, starting at Albert Lea, Minnesota, and the Fort Dodge & Fort Ridgeley Railroad and Telegraph Company from Fort Dodge. The line became part of the M&StL in 1881. The M&StL was acquired by the Chicago & North Western Railway in 1960, and much of its former trackage was later abandoned. This line was abandoned in 1981, except for the small bit of track in Forest City.

Just north of here is the Winnebago Industries manufacturing complex. Today, the company manufactures both Winnebago and Itasca motorhomes.

According to the Winnebago website, "In the mid-1950s Forest City, Iowa, was looking at a bleak future. The farm economy was down and young people were leaving this rural area. Forward-looking members of the community set about bringing industry to town. In 1958, businessman John K. Hanson and others convinced a California company to open a travel trailer factory in Forest City. After a rough start, the operation was purchased by five Forest City residents and John K. Hanson became president. In 1960 the name of the company was changed to Winnebago Industries." In 1966, the first motor home rolled off the Winnebago Industries assembly lines. The Itasca line was introduced in 1975. In 2008, as the company celebrated its 50th anniversary, Winnebago Industries reached another milestone with the production of the 400,000th unit.

75.8 **COUNTY LINE** – To the south is **Hancock County**, while to the north is **Winnebago County**. The Winnebago tribe lived in this area. The name reportedly means "men of the bad-smelling waters."

Winnebago County was created in the 1850-51 Legislature of the State of Iowa, which defined the boundaries of the county. The land for the new county came from Fayette County. Due to the small population and lack of its own government, the county was initially managed by Polk County. In 1853, the county became attached to Webster County. It wasn't until the fall of 1857 that Winnebago County became completely independent.

The county is Iowa's second-smallest county by area and had a population of 10,679 during the 2020 census, down about 200 residents over the past decade. The county's population actually peaked in 1940 with 13,972 residents. Much of the population decline is due to the mechanization of farming where one tractor does the work of hundreds of mules and workers.

The county seat of Winnebago County is Forest City.

76.0 END OF TRACK – This is the current end of track, located just south of the location of the former CRIP station. The railroad was abandoned beyond Forest City to Buffalo Center during the early 1980s.

76.1 FOREST CITY – Forest City was CRIP milepost 157.5. The track no longer comes all the way downtown, once the site of a one-story stucco station. The Rock Island depot was located on the west side of the mainline between I and J Streets, five blocks west of the courthouse and about ten blocks west of the Minneapolis & St. Louis depot. The freight house was a block to the south, with A. M. Clauson's elevator and coal yards across the tracks to the east.

In 1901 this same area on the siding to the east was P. M. Ingold's grain elevator (10,000 bushels and built in 1895) and to its north the Charles Ripple elevator (the same size and also built in 1895), coal bins and corn cribs. Maps from 1913 show that both elevators had changed ownership, with Ripple's elevator being the Jeska & Clauson's elevator, and the Ingold elevator being the Smith-Wright & Sons facility. Further north was the Forest City Canning Company, also served by the Rock Island.

In March 1856, Robert Clark laid out the town of Forest City, at a location described as being where a river flowed, trees were plentiful, and a prairie full of deer, elk and buffalo was to the west. Robert Clark was reportedly the first settler in the area that became Forest City, and he later became the first shop owner, the first postmaster, and later a county judge. Forest City, although it is located in the southern part of Winnebago County about one-half a mile from the south line and nearly seven miles from the eastern boundary, soon became the county seat. A sawmill opened here in September 1856, and just before the first train arrived the first elevator was built in Forest City in 1879. The arrival of the railroad also brought northern European emigrants, most from places like Sweden, Norway, Denmark and Germany.

The community was called Big Brush and Hill City before the name was changed to reflect the timber in the area. Forest City became the Winnebago County seat in 1858. It was incorporated on June 14, 1878. In 1879, the community campaigned to bring the Minneapolis & St. Louis Railroad to Forest City. Today, Forest City calls itself "the smallest big town in Iowa" and is the headquarters of Winnebago Industries, a manufacturer of motor homes founded by local resident John K. Hanson. The population in 2010 was 4151.

Forest City is also the home of Puckerbrush Days, an annual festival. The name is unique and believed to be the only festival using the name in the United States. The festival name comes from a bush that once grew around the town, known as the Puckerbrush. The bush had a berry on it that when eaten, made people pucker: thus, its name. The bush no longer grows in the area, but the name and its legend is carried on by the annual festival.

This 1916 Sanborn map shows the Rock Island depot and water tower, once located in the open block south and east of the intersection of South Best and West J Street. *Sanborn Fire Insurance Map from Forest City, Winnebago County, Iowa.* Sanborn Map Company, August 1916. Map. Retrieved from the Library of Congress, https://www.loc.gov/item/sanborn02660_004/.

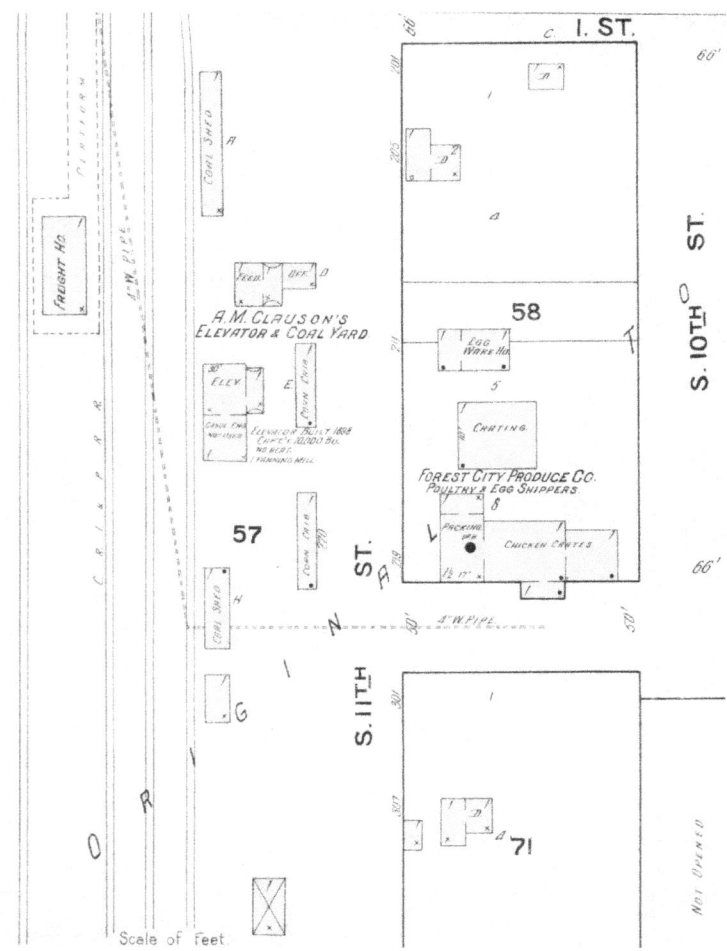

South of West I Street was the Rock Island Freight House. On the east side of the tracks was A. M. Clauson's elevator and coal yards, as shown on this 1916 Sanborn map. *Sanborn Fire Insurance Map from Forest City, Winnebago County, Iowa.* Sanborn Map Company, August 1916. Map. Retrieved from the Library of Congress, https://www.loc.gov/item/sanborn02660_004/.

Former Minneapolis & St. Louis Line

75.1 **FOREST CITY** – This is the official milepost for Forest City. To the east is a connection to a short piece of M&StL track that serves an agricultural facility. A description of what remains of this line is included here.

According to several early histories of Forest City and Winnebago County, the Minnesota & Iowa Southern Railway Company was organized at Forest City on April 27, 1878. The plans were to build a railroad from Minnesota and south across Iowa, passing through Forest City. The plan eventually consolidated into the Minneapolis & St. Louis Railway. This line is the result of those plans.

The Twenty Eighth Annual Report of the Railroad and Commission of The State of Minnesota (1913) had a report that clarifies the incorporation and plans. The report stated that "The Minnesota & Iowa Southern Railroad Company was an Iowa corporation, created under the general laws of Iowa, in 1878. The Fort Dodge & Fort Ridgley Railroad Company was an Iowa corporation, incorporated under the general laws of Iowa, on July 24, 1876. On April 20, 1881, the Minneapolis & St. Louis Railway Company, the Minneapolis & Duluth Railroad Company, the Minnesota & Iowa Southern and the Fort Dodge & Fort Ridgley Companies were consolidated into one company by the name of The Minneapolis & St. Louis Railway Company, a railroad corporation of Minnesota and Iowa."

The plan was generally successful, and the first train arrived at Forest City at 3:30 pm on December 10, 1879 (some sources say December 3, 1879). However, they all agree that the day was cold and stormy. The railroad also built a telegraph, and the first message was sent over the line on Christmas Day 1879, sent by Forest City Mayor Secor to officials at Lake Mills, Iowa.

As what became the Rock Island was being built to Forest City, a line was built from Hayfield Junction to Hayfield, Iowa. This provided a connection with what became the Minneapolis & St. Louis. For a time, trains ran over this line from Hayfield, also known as Madison, to Forest City, until the Garner-Forest City line opened in 1895.

The Minneapolis & St. Louis route eventually became part of the Chicago & North Western, which abandoned the line through Forest City in March 1981.

75.3 4TH STREET – This is where the connecting track enters the former route of the Minneapolis & St. Louis. For the old M&StL, this was Milepost 153.7. To the east is a large RV park known as the Winnebago Rally Grounds. It is here that the Winnebago International Travelers (WIT) Club holds its annual Grand National Rally, drawing an average of 1000 units. To the west is the large Winnebago assembly complex.

Heading north, the rail line follows U.S. Highway 69 along the east side of Forest City.

76.3 EAST G STREET – The south switch of the siding to the west is located just north of this grade crossing. This end of the siding is often known as the Fertilizer Pit Track.

76.4 **EAST J STREET** – Just south of this grade crossing is the former Minneapolis & St. Louis station, today a simple building with a flat roof. In 1960, the station had train signals to alert crews to the need to pick up orders at the station, There was also a large sign on the roof stating "Forest City – Minneapolis & St. Louis Railway." A large Railway Express Agency sign was also on each end of the building. Today, the building is painted gray with red trim and has been restored with Minneapolis & St. Louis lettering.

To the north is the reason this line still survives – the Farmers Cooperative Association. The co-op was created at the Winnebago County Courthouse in 1916. The Association has operations in Forest City and Leland, Iowa; Kiester, Minnesota; and a bin site west of Forest City. In April 2016, Farmers Co-op acquired Main Fertilizer adding facilities in Buffalo Center, Iowa, and Winnebago, Minnesota. Agriculture is important here, and Winnebago County reportedly produces the largest corn yield per acre of any Iowa county.

Maps from 1901 show that the Seibert Brothers & Company grain elevator (20,000-bushel capacity built in 1896) and the Citizens Elevator Company (21,000-bushel capacity and built in 1898) were just north of East J Street. To their north was a large set of stock pens. By 1913, the Henry Denzel Grain Company had an elevator here and the others were not shown on maps from that era.

The north end of the Iowa Northern's Garner Subdivision is marked by this Minneapolis & St. Louis Railway depot at Forest City, Iowa.

76.7 END OF TRACK – The line ends just south of the Winnebago River, where a 352-foot bridge was required to cross the stream. This was once M&StL Milepost 152.3.

About the Author

Barton Jennings grew up in Arkansas, spending years exploring the various railroad lines throughout the state. He has written numerous articles for magazines like *Trains*, *Railfan & Railroad*, and *Pacific Rail News*. He has also written books about railroads across the county such as the Arkansas & Missouri; the Iowa Interstate; the Alaska Railroad; and the Rock Island's Choctaw Route.

Additionally, for almost three decades, Barton Jennings has been organizing charter passenger trains and writing the route descriptions, both for planning purposes and for the enjoyment of the passengers. These trips have been in all areas of the United States, often covering operations that haven't seen a passenger train in decades. He has also had the pleasure of riding the trips of other organizations, including trips over the Iowa Northern Railway, where some of the material for this book was collected.

His house has several rooms full of books, timetables and other documents about this and other railroads – important research items from a time long before today's internet. Today, Bart Jennings, after years working in the railroad industry, is a professor emeritus of supply chain management and teaches transportation operations. He also still teaches regulatory issues for the railroad industry, a way to stay in touch with the industry he loves.